To Wendy with my
love and respect for
all times!

Misconceptions and Simple Truths
in
Dressage

H. L. M. van Schaik

Misconceptions and Simple Truths in Dressage

J. A. Allen
London

British Library Cataloguing in Publication Data

Schaik, H. L. M. van
   Misconceptions and simple truths in dressage.
   1. Dressage
   I. Title
   636.1'0886   SF309.5

ISBN 0–85131–417–1

Published in Great Britain in 1986 by
J. A. Allen & Company Limited,
1, Lower Grosvenor Place, Buckingham Palace Road,
London, SW1W 0EL

Book production Bill Ireson

Filmset by Fakenham Photosetting Limited, Fakenham, Norfolk

Printed by St Edmundsbury Press, Bury St Edmunds, Suffolk

Contents

Geleitwort

Was hier dem Leser angeboten wird, ist ein auf wohlfundiertem Wissen ruhender, mit vielen gezielten Hinweisen auf die Schwachstellen gespickter Zusammenschnitt der "klassischen Grundgesetze" der Reitkunst. In allen Epochen hat ihre Beachtung Kunstwerke entstehen lassen, die zwar nie ein Menschen- und manchmal nur ein Pferdeleben zu überdauern vermochten, die aber trotzdem einen festen Platz in der Geschichte der Reitkunst behalten haben.

Der Verfasser ist ein glühender Anhänger dieser Kunst, und daher geht es ihm bei seinen Aussagen in erster Linie darum, auf die hohen Werte hinzuweisen, die in dieser Kunst beheimatet sind. Sie zählt zu jenen Künsten, die ihre Impulse nicht von der ungeheuren Motorik unserer schnellebigen Zeit empfängt, sondern im Gegenteil den Menschen eher zwingen sollte, mit Rücksicht auf seinen Partner Pferd das Tempo jenen von letzteren diktierten Gesetzen anzupassen.

Wie mir scheint, will hier der Verfasser aber nicht anklagen, sondern mit seinen Aussagen nur aufzeigen, um wieviel Schönes und Erhabenes sich sowohl der Reiter selbst bringt aber natürlich auch jener erwartungsvolle Betrachter gebracht wird, wenn die gemeinsame Leistung nicht mehr von der Harmonie des Zusammenspiels, sondern nur noch vom ergeizigen Denken des Menschen diktiert wird. Es gehen damit nicht nur die der Kunst als wichtige Basis dienenden Grundsätze verloren, sondern mehr und mehr wird sie für den Außenstehenden uninteressant und damit geht langsam aber auch ihre Anziehungskraft, die sie eh und je hatte, verloren.

Wenn diese Schrift auch in erster Linie für den Fachmann bestimmt ist und einen oder den anderen von ihnen zum Nachdenken bewegen soll, wird sie auch den nur am Rande an der Materie Interessierten etwas zu sagen und gerade letzterem den Blick für die Unterschiede zu schärfen vermögen. Um echte Reitkunst von reiner Erfolgshysterie unterscheiden zu können, bedarf es viel weninger eines großen Fachwissens, als der Bereitschaft, die Komponenten dieser Kunst auf sich wirken zu lassen.

Es sei daher dem Verfasser für diesen Dienst ehrlich gedankt. Seine Aussagen haben umso mehr Gewicht, als sie auf persönlich Erlebtem und Erarbeitetem beruhen und daher mit hoher Oberzeugungskraft ausgestattet sind.

BRIGADIER-GENERAL KURT ALBRECHT

Foreword (translation)

Here the reader is offered a poignant cross-section of the "classical principles" of the art of riding, based on a very sound background of knowledge. This perspective is established through the use of many telling examples of the art's weaknesses. In every era works of art were created through acknowledgement of the art. These works of art never lived longer than a human life, sometimes not longer than one horse's life. Nevertheless, they have held a secure place in the history of the art of riding.

The author is a fervent fan of this art, and therefore his main purpose is to emphasise the high values that are within this art. Classical riding should be one of those arts unaffected by the monstrous drive of today's fast pace. In fact, this art should force us to choose a tempo that fits the high standards for consideration of our partner, the horse.

It appears to me that the author is not accusing with his comments, but rather pointing out how much beauty for both rider and hopeful spectator is lost when man's ambitious drive dictates what should transpire between horse and rider rather than letting the harmony in the combined effort of the two parties be the guide. Ironically, not only do the classical principles get lost with this ambitious drive but also the interest and fascination of the spectators.

Although this book is perhaps speaking more directly to the professional and may move one or the other to ponder, it will also appeal to those only marginally interested and will sharpen their ability to see the differences mentioned. It takes much less riding expertise to see the difference between real art in riding and pure ambition than it takes readiness to let the components of the art touch you through your senses.

I honestly thank the author for this service. His statements carry that much more weight and conviction because they are based on personal experience.

BRIGADIER-GENERAL KURT ALBRECHT, *former Director of the Spanish Riding School*

Acknowledgements

This book would never have been embarked upon without the help of many people.

Through the provocation of Jean-Marc Oppenheim I began this endeavour. He brought order to the chaos of articles I had written for different publications over the years and persuaded me to make a book out of them.

Stephanie Grant took the next step and made the tentative layout of the book by organising the different articles in chapters. She made several very valuable suggestions in the preparatory stages. Frances Ecker-Rasz did the final editing and also aided me in the completion stages of the text with her valuable suggestions and her expertise. Carol Selikowitz did all the technical photographs, not only by pressing the button on her camera but also by making the decisions on how she wanted them taken. Her talent included the reproductions of some of my older photographs and all of the processing. Sheila McLevedge, my assistant since 1974, posed for the pictures, did the artwork for the line drawings and has been a patient listener and sharp critic when I rambled on about my ideas. Walter Carrington and Daniel Pevsner introduced me to the Alexander Technique and made me understand the importance of the use of the abdominal muscles in order to acquire a functional and elegant position on the horse.

I feel very indebted to all these good friends.

That Brigadier-General Kurt Albrecht, former Director of the Spanish Riding School, was willing to write the Foreword is a great honour, for which I feel very grateful.

List of Illustrations

It is not necessary to have expectations in order to start something, neither to be successful in order to persevere

WILLIAM OF ORANGE

Introduction

Unity in the movement of man and horse is the goal of equitation, the art of riding. Without this unity no movements in high collection are possible, and this unity is only possible when there is a mutual confidence between man and horse. For those who are bewildered by all of the complicated theories and the contradictory methods in achieving such unity, I have in this book tried to focus on a few basic truths which, when really understood, will help dissolve misconceptions and show the way to classical equitation and also to the modern concept of riding. Whenever man confronts the horse, he should try to inspire confidence. This begins when handling the young animal, continues while schooling, and later while using the horse for work. Therefore, take your time: don't hurt the horse by being brusque, don't fall in the saddle when mounting, and don't yank in the reins. Don't forget the horse has to adapt himself to the task of carrying the rider. With a young horse, allow the muscles to develop, the bones to grow, and the tendons and ligaments to become strong.

I won't go into detail because there are many excellent books describing the handling and the schooling of the young horse. The reason that I mention these things is that there are also books written advocating a quick and easy way. There is no such thing as a quick and easy way in equitation. Physical development takes time, and all through history the great masters of equitation have been concerned with schooling the horse in such a way that he is able to carry a rider with the least wear for himself and the most comfort for the rider, while developing the horses' muscles in such a way that he is physically able to be obedient in executing the movements required. The horse needs a lot of gymnastic exercise to enable him to redistribute his weight, without which no movements in equitation are possible. When we ask movements of a horse which he cannot make because his muscles are not yet developed, we not only ruin him physically but also mentally.

In the early 1960s, I started writing, off and on, articles about certain aspects of the movements asked for in dressage tests. I enjoy judging, but especially at the lower levels it gives me a feeling of frustration. Most of the people riding in those tests try very hard and do their utmost, but most of the time it is all wrong, because they don't really know what they are supposed to do. It is impossible, considering the time and space, to explain in the commentary on the score sheet why so many things are wrong, and what should be done to correct them, so in my articles I tried to explain several of the problems. The first part of this book deals with special problems and is based on those articles, though they have been rewritten, expanded and enlarged; new problems have been dealt with as well.

The Reflections (Chapter 13) are based on articles I wrote after attending international dressage shows. The first article was written after I had watched the European Dressage Championships in Wolfsburg in 1969. I was very disappointed, and the more I travelled and the more I saw, the more my concern for the future of classical dressage grew. Erich Glahn had warned in 1956 against the dangers that were threatening classical equitation. In 1974 Miss Oehlert, a pupil of Egon von Neindorff, asked in an article in the German magazine *Sankt Georg* if the art of riding should be sacrificed to dressage sport. I always had hoped that people more qualified than I and more able to express their thoughts would come to the fore to defend classical equitation, but nobody did. There are an increasing number of people who sense that there is something wrong with the way dressage is going. Those people gave me the inspiration to continue to write and to try to find out what is really wrong with the modern interpretation of classical equitation. I hoped eventually to find the ways to correct the wrongs as a result of my reflections after the 1984 Olympic Games in Los Angeles. I have come up with a series of possible solutions that may save classical equitation, and these are gathered at the end of the Reflections.

Elegance on horseback consists of a straight and free position as a result of a well balanced body; as a result the rider maintains, during all the movements the horse makes, without losing his seat, as much as he is able to, in an appropriate balance, an air of comfort and freedom, which makes him an elegant rider

LA GUÉRINIÈRE

1 The Rider's Position

When Louis XIII began his riding lessons with Antoine de Pluvinel, the first thing he asked was, "What do you expect first of your pupil?" De Pluvinel answered, "That he be an elegant rider." ("Qu'il soit bel homme de cheval.") The King then asked: "What distinction do you make between an elegant rider and a good rider (bon homme de cheval)?" To this de Pluvinel answered, "I make a great distinction because it would be very embarrassing to be a good rider without being an elegant rider. It is, however, possible to be an elegant rider without being a good rider." This conversation took place during the 17th century when, of course, nobody had ever heard of dressage competitions. Unfortunately, today it is a fact that elegant riders are seen rarely, and that good riders are not at all embarrassed by the fact that they are very often not elegant riders. This is a pity, because I am convinced that the functionally correct position is an elegant position.

The position is functionally correct when the rider does not disturb the horse, and when he is able to give the aids in a discreet but emphatic way, at the correct moment, to the correct spot and in the correct strength. The rider will not disturb the horse when he has an independent seat. He does not have to use the reins to stay on the horse; his hands are totally independent of the movements of the horse; he never has "dancing hands"; and he never yanks the horse in the mouth because of an unexpected movement. Having an independent seat means also that the rider is able to move in unison with the movement of the horse, and to keep his own centre of gravity as much as possible in line with the horse's centre of gravity. The rider sits at all times as lightly as possible on the horse, for it is evident that the less of a burden the rider is for the horse, the better the horse can perform.

How does the rider achieve this independent seat that allows him to be at one with the movement of the horse and to give the correct aids at all times?

When I first arrived in America I was bewildered by all the

different seats people were talking about. My reaction to this was to say: "There is but one seat, the correct seat." One could qualify this by calling it the balanced seat, because in riding balance is fundamental. The rider should not fall off his horse, because he is in balance and not because he hangs on the reins, or grabs with his thighs and knees. Should the rider resort to these emergency movements, then he makes himself stiff, he tightens up and therefore he never can be in balance. In order to be able to feel what is going on and to react in the correct way, the rider has to be in balance on his horse.

It is commonly accepted that the rider should sit straight, that there should be one line from shoulders to seat-bones to heels and that he should be plumb on his seat-bones. Here is where the difficulties start. Sitting straight on a chair and sitting straight on a horse are two totally different positions. When we sit upright on a chair, we sit on the foremost part of the seat-bones, and when we stretch to be straight we hollow the lumbar part of the spine. On a horse we should sit on the back part of the seat-bones.

If the rider sits on the horse the way he sits on a chair, his knees will be too high; he will sit partly on his thighs and the upper body will be behind the vertical line of shoulders, seat-bones, heels. He will also sit too close to the cantle; thus his centre of gravity is not aligned with the horse's centre of gravity. All this results in the rider not being able to influence the horse properly.

It is difficult to achieve the correct position, and it is difficult to explain it. In no other walk of life do we have to adopt a position which takes our shoulders and heels back and tilts our pelvis forward and upward. A French author, as a consequence, once said: "Man was not created to ride on horseback."

We have seen that on a horse we should sit on the back part of the seat-bones. In this position the pelvis is then tilted forward and upward (the seat-bones being part of the pelvis).

The best way to achieve this position is to make oneself tall. The Alexander Technique taught me that to achieve this is to engage the abdominal muscles, taking a very deep breath starting in the lower part of the abdomen. When one does this with totally decontracted shoulders, the sternum goes up, and one feels oneself becoming taller. Becoming taller stretches the back and straightens the lordosis, the hollow that everybody has at the small of the back. It also gives the pelvis the right tilt forward and upward, and pushes the seat-bones into the saddle.

When one tries to sit straight, the emphasis should be put on the functioning of the abdominal muscles and not on the back. The advantage of using the abdominal muscles is that it prevents "belly dancing" (the constant back and forth motion of the pelvis) and bobbing of the head. It also prevents the small of the back from becoming hollow, and it influences the tone of the leg muscles. There was a time when a straight back meant a hollow back. A hollow back is functionally incorrect, because it causes internal stresses as well as rigidity. There are many people who believe that belly dancing is a proof of suppleness. This is a misconception, because this movement is only possible when the abdominal muscles are not engaged. When used correctly, the abdominals are responsible for the independent and balanced seat that we believe is the most influential on the horse and also the most elegant. The abdominals are not only a powerful help to, but also a discreet way of, creating impulsion. Belly dancing in the saddle is not only functionally incorrect, but also unaesthetic.

In order to prevent the rider from sitting on the end of his spine, thereby curving the small of the back, the angle of the hip-joint has to be widened, and the knees have to go down. There should be a little bend in the knee-joint; in this way it is not difficult to achieve the line: shoulders, seat-bones, heels. The rider should be very careful not to bring the knees too deep, as this will put him on the front part of the seat-bone, even on the pubic-bone. In order to prevent the knees from being too straight, the rider should make sure that the lumbar part of his spine is upright and that the lower legs are not too far back.

The elegant rider who sits correctly should have his head up; he should look over the world. When the chin drops, the head follows and the spine collapses. The Alexander Technique taught me that the head has to be balanced. In other words, the rider should have his head balanced without the use of muscles. Using these muscles to keep the chin up creates tensions and gives the appearance of a "bull neck". On a horse one should avoid any kind of rigidity, because correct riding implies a great deal of reacting to what one is feeling, and being rigid makes feeling what goes on with the horse impossible. Therefore, balance your head; do not force it up.

The elbows should be slightly bent. This, with free shoulders will guarantee an elastic contact with the horse's mouth. Elasticity is impossible with stretched elbows and a narrow chest. There should be one line; elbows, fists, mouth. If the hands are below this line, pressure will be put on the bars of the horse's mouth, and the head will go up. If the hands come above the line elbow, mouth, the horse will come behind the bit.

The rider should never use his biceps. If he does, he will lock the elbow-joint, resulting in a dead hand. When the rider wants to resist he should use his abdominal muscles, his back muscles and his triceps, thus increasing the weight in the reins. He should *never* pull. Nor should he squeeze with his thighs. If he does, he cannot use his lower legs to give the aids correctly. His lower legs should stick as Seunig once put it "like wet towels" to the horse's barrel. In this way they are always in place, ready to be used when necessary. The rider should pull his toes up and have light contact with the stirrup irons. If his heels are pushed down, there is too much pressure on the irons and his lower legs will tend to go forward. If a rider has the tendency to always ride with the lower legs too far back, then the correction is to ask the rider to push his heels down. The knee-joint and the ankle-joint should never be locked. They function as shock absorbers, and when they are locked, they cannot function as such.

When the rider has to mount a young or unschooled horse for the first time, mount a horse with a cold back, or when he rides a horse over cavalletti, it is advisable to keep his seat-bones out of the saddle by putting his body weight on his thighs and on the stirrup irons. The rider brings his body slightly forward, being sure to use his abdominal muscles in order to keep his balance.

To recapitulate: The rider should keep his sternum up, using his abdominal muscles; this prevents "belly dancing" and a bobbing head. His chest should be wide, and his shoulders free. He should never forget that the small of the back has to be upright, never hollow, which is difficult because the lordosis is naturally hollow. The rider should be forward in the saddle in order to be in line with the centre of gravity of the horse. The rider should sit deep in the saddle and not on top of the saddle; he should have his knees deep, resulting in a maximum of contact with the horse's barrel. As the French say: "The more contact with the leg, the more control over the hindquarters." However, if the knee is too deep, the legs go too far back, and the rider is no longer on the back part of the seat-bones, with the result that the rider has no influence on the horse.

Postscript

Recently the adepts of the Martial Arts have shown interest in riding. While both the Martial Arts and the Alexander Technique stress the importance of "breathing" there is a danger of serious confusion. While the Alexander Technique puts the emphasis on inhaling, as explained above, the Martial Arts put the emphasis on exhaling. There is a reason for this. The fighter has to be solid on the ground, for this he has to drop his centre of gravity, he has to be "rooting" in the soil. In order to achieve this he has to exhale. By exhaling the fighter tightens the abdominal muscles, thus protecting the internal organs. I have been told that Muhammed Ali took lessons at a Kung Fu school to learn to tighten his abdominal muscles when he was against the ropes and thus would be able to endure the pounding his opponent was giving him. When the opponent got tired, Ali was able to counterattack. He called this "the rope-a-dope". The fighter yells when attacking, not to intimidate his opponent, but to tighten his abdominal muscles. The skier also needs to be solid on the ground, for that reason he lowers his centre of gravity.

In riding it is the horse who needs to be solid on the ground. We teach him this, not by inhaling or exhaling, but by making him get his hindlegs under the load, so that the hindlegs will not only propel but also carry. This will enable the horse to carry himself. The rider will be solid on the horse when he is in complete balance, being one with the movement of the horse. In this way he will be as little of a burden as possible. How to achieve this has been described earlier. If a rider exhales, thinking that this will put him more solidly on the horse, he will be in the "brace the backbone" position (see above) and he will make himself quite a burden for the horse. There are those who claim that during the piaffe they exhale. When one realises that during this movement the horse with very springy

23

strides gets the hindquarters under and elevates the shoulders, it is clear that the horse can only do this if he has the unobstructed use of his back muscles. It is also clear that if the rider exhales, he makes himself heavy, he hampers the use of the horse's back muscles and thereby makes it impossible for the horse to execute a brilliant piaffe.

The principle lies in collaboration. Quiet, subtle constraint gives way to gentle marital servitude, which implies a conquest, properly progressive of the body and the soul of the spouse. And upon achievement of this intimacy the rider succeeds in making himself understood by touches, signs and brainwaves

SOBÈNE OLSTEF

2 Natural Reactions

One of the reasons why learning to ride is so difficult is that the natural reactions can be dangerous, or at least counterproductive when one is riding a horse. Being frightened by something unexpected causes one to cringe, perhaps a remnant from times when we lived in the wilderness and our first reaction to being threatened was to make ourselves small. On a horse, this reaction is the surest way of being deposed.

When a horse moves off, the rider's natural reaction is to hang on to the reins, to lean forward with the knees and the heels up, with the result that the horse wants to go even faster. The rider's trained reaction should be to relax the seat and leg muscles, retain an upright position and give with the hands. An example of the effectiveness of giving is: when a jockey on the flat wants to slow down, he gives with his hands and when he wants to go faster he takes hold of the reins. Remaining in an upright position prevents the rider falling forward and over the horse's neck or just from falling off. The relaxation of the seat and leg muscles calms the horse by removing a cause of tension.

To turn a horse a rider will naturally pull his rein in the direction he wants to go towards his body and yield with the outside rein. I call this technique "riding the bicycle". If you do this there is a very good chance that, should the horse not want to go in the direction you want him to, he will throw himself on the outside shoulder and move off in the opposite direction.

If, for example, the horse does not want to go to the left, he will throw himself on the right shoulder, taking the opportunity offered by the rider who is hanging on the left rein. A very common example of this situation occurs in an indoor arena when a horse becomes frightened of noises or a shadow on the wall and tries to get off the wall by throwing himself over the inside shoulder. Most riders will pull on the outside rein to try to keep the horse on the wall. Because the rider pulls the horse's head to the outside, to the wall, bending to face the outside, he helps the horse to move to the inside of the arena. What the rider should do in a case like this, as soon as he feels that there is going to be trouble, is to close the inside leg on the girth, which often gives confidence to the horse. The inner leg in this situation should never be put behind the girth, because this would push the hindquarters to the outside, thus helping the horse to go over the inside shoulder.

If the rider feels that the horse is really upset, he should close his inside leg and, at the same time, he should bring his inside arm up as high as possible with a stretched elbow, pressing the inner rein against the horse's neck as a kind of a barrier. The outside rein should have about the same tension as the inside rein, so that it can function as a counterweight. This will prevent the horse from going over the inside shoulder, because in this way the rider bends the horse around his inside leg. The high hand tilts the lower part of the head sideways and upward, which has an effect on the last two vertebrae of the horse's neck (atlas axis). The elbow has to be stretched because the more the force applied goes up, and not backwards towards the rider's body, the less interference there will be with the forward movement. In a situation like this, it is vital that the horse keeps moving. In case the rider has been too late with the leg and the high hand, and the horse is already over the shoulder, away from the wall, the rider has to try to make a circle to the inside. The best way to do this is to use opening rein, making the horse bend around the rider's inside leg. The rider should keep the horse on the circle until the horse surrenders and bends. Then the rider should take the horse back to the wall, the inside hand high and maintaining the bend; this is a kind of rough, pragmatic shoulder-in; the horse should not be allowed to look to the outside. By applying this technique the rider has put the horse on the aids and has created a barrier to prevent the horse from moving away from the spot he is afraid of.

It is of course true that one should let the horse look at what frightens him. But it is a misconception that one can do this by pulling on the rein on the side of the frightening object. When one wants to show the horse the object of his fears, then go at it in a straight line and keep the horse straight by enclosing the neck between the reins. If possible, begin to walk in a straight line towards the object from a point approximately three horse-lengths away. Make frequent halts and caress the horse, making sure that he stays straight. The closer the object, the longer the halts and the petting should last. Allow the horse to sniff at what scared him. Once there, he very likely will have no further interest.

It is of the utmost importance that the rider changes his natural reactions, adapting them to the new situation of sitting on a horse. Only when the rider has trained his reactions will he be able to develop an independent seat. This will enable him to use the aids correctly, in an elastic and feeling way, and not mechanically.

Unqualified disobedience is a frequent misconception, when the rider is not only demanding but not listening to the horse. If the horse is a strong personality the result is a notoriously resistant animal; if the horse has a submissive, weak personality, it can be brainwashed into a mechanical automat, a zombie. Both are contrary to correct dressage

TIBOR PADANYI

A good hand is the one that can resist and yield when necessary and receive with precision the action created by the legs

SALOMON DE LA BROUE

3 The Aids

The word "aids" derives from to aid, to help. In French the word is "les aides"; in German "die Hilfen"; in Dutch "de hulpen". Xenophon used a word with an overall meaning of "to indicate". Since I want to stress the fact that the idea of helping the horse permeates the whole literature of equitation, I need to make a short digression into history.

When man made the transition from eating the horse to using him, it was to be expected that in the beginning there was fear on both sides. Man feared the horse because he was strong and unpredictable; the horse feared man because he hurt him and tried to constrain him. I presume that once man tried to use the horse, some patient people found out that the horse is not an aggressive animal, but that he can become aggressive when constrained and treated in a cruel way. Perhaps this was the beginning of psychological insight.

By Xenophon's time (380 B C) a lot of progress had been made in achieving a more balanced relationship between man and horse, changing from antagonism to co-operation. Xenophon makes this clear: "One should never lose one's temper in treating the horse; this is the one best precept and custom in dealing with horses ... Those who compel the horse with blows make him more frightened than ever."

There were, and are to this day, frequent relapses. Federigo Grisone in his *Gli Ordini di Cavalcare* (1550), does not forget to reward and can be very gentle. However, because he believes that there are vicious horses, he can also be very cruel: he advocates hitting the horse around the ears, letting a cat, tied with its back up against a pole, crawl over the belly and between the hindlegs of the horse. When a horse does not want to move forward Grisone holds burning straw under its tail.

To this day there are still those who consider the horse to be the opponent. They claim that if the horse does not offer a fight, the rider should provoke one so that the horse knows who is the boss.

They do not seem to realise that if the horse wins the fight, they have lost the horse; if they win the fight, they have a mechanised, cowed horse without brilliance. In this vein we may learn something from de Pluvinel, who wrote: ". . . you must be careful not to bore him or snuff out his gentleness. Because, as with the bloom on fruit, so with horses, once it is lost it is gone forever and once the gentleness is lost one can never regain it." De Pluvinel goes on to say that when one has no consideration for one's horse, one either loses the horse's gentleness or makes him incorrectably vicious.

De Pluvinel was not the only one to understand that it makes no sense to wage battle with the horse. Long before him, Abou Bekr, master of the horse of Sultan Nacer of Egypt around 1300 said: "Schooling based on gentleness and psychology should aim at developing useful qualities by making use of the qualities the horse is born with."

Salomon de la Broue, a contemporary of de Pluvinel, wrote in *Le Cavalerice françois* (1594): "If a horse refuses or holds back this is not so much caused by malice as well as by the fear of being punished, not knowing for what cause." In the same book he wrote: "I claim that there will be disorder, resulting in a stiff back, a hard mouth and fear and sooner or later he'll become rebellious, if one tries to put his head and neck in the correct position, before the horse has learned to freely turn."

As one delves into the history of equitation, two things become clear. On the one hand a lot of progress has been made in man's attitude towards the horse and there is a lot more co-operation than antagonism. Also, techniques of how to make clear to the horse what we want him to do have been considerably refined. On the other hand, however, it is clear that either because of the mentality of some people, or through lack of understanding in how to deal with the horse, a lot of aggressive practices, such as mentioned in the above quotations, still continue. After this historical intermezzo, let's return to the subject, the aids.

When one looks at any group of riders, it is very clear that the gravest sins are committed with the hands. The main reasons for this are the natural reactions, mentioned in the preceding chapter. Everybody will tell you that you have to have light and elastic contact, and that you should never pull. But practically nobody has elastic contact, and most people pull. It is appalling to see how many people ride with stretched elbows, their hands halfway up the horse's neck, making it impossible for the horse to move freely and without constraint. (Especially in the beginning of a lesson one should give the horse enough room so that he can move without being constrained.) I am convinced that practically all of the problems with the horse's head are caused by bad hands. It is very difficult to decide when resisting becomes pulling. For this one has to understand the function of the arm muscles.

In books written during the heyday of military riding, one reads that the hands should be at a certain height and that the elbows should be rigid against the body. Before the First World War instruction was practically always given on schooled horses, who carried themselves. In such circumstances, a play of the fingers and a little movement of the wrist was all that was needed to guide the horse. But those horses are not available for instruction nowadays. It is very important that the rider does not constrain the horse; in other words that he does not impede the forward movement of the horse. Therefore, sitting in the functionally correct position the rider should follow, in the walk, the movement of the horse's head. He should surrender his hands to the horse, maintaining a featherlight contact with the horse's mouth. In this way the rider will get the feel of the horse's rhythm. The hands should stay in a line that includes the elbow, lower arm, hand, rein and the horse's mouth. If the hands come above that line, the horse will come behind the bit; if the hands come below that line, the head will go up. The wrist should be straight and unbroken. Only well schooled horses who have learned to carry themselves can be ridden with the wrist and the fingers.

When the rider wants to restrain the horse, he should make it more difficult for the horse to bring his head forward by tightening the elastic contact, not by using the biceps, which I call "putting on the handbrake". If the rider uses the biceps, he locks the elbow-joint, making elasticity impossible and resulting in a hand that is not able to yield. Also, the rider should never use the muscles in his lower arms. This is very important in order to avoid dancing hands in the trot. The hands have to be balanced, moved only by the horse and not by the rider's body movement. When the muscles of the lower arm are contracted, it is impossible to balance the hands. (Remember what the lower arm does when you try to balance a stick on your index finger.)

If the rider cannot use the muscles of his lower arm, nor his biceps, what does he do to restrain the horse by putting more weight on the reins? The answer is he must use his abdominal and back muscles, his triceps and pectoralis major, the muscles one uses when one expands the rib cage when taking a deep breath. It is evident that one can do this only from the independent, balanced seat.

There was a time when it was said that a rider had to use his back in order to ride correctly, in order to influence the horse in the most efficient way. This has caused a lot of misunderstanding. People thought that this meant that the rider had to lean backward in order to get the seat deeper into the saddle, that the rider had to make himself heavy. These are disastrous presumptions. How can one expect the horse to function well if the rider sits too heavily and does not align his own centre of gravity with that of the horse? The less one is a burden for the horse, the better he can serve us. Riding with the back means that by using the abdominal muscles and thereby stretching the spine one creates impulsion, and by using the back muscles in combination with the triceps one can increase and decrease the weight on the reins.

In discussing the natural reactions, I pointed to the adverse possibilities when, in making a turn, the rider pulls on the inside rein, or in other words, when he uses the direct rein of opposition. This example was the pragmatic reason never to use this rein. In schooling horses, one should be well aware of the fact that when being ridden most horses try not to use their backs. There are various theories as to why this is. It is my conviction that this stiffness is man-made. Most horses, and especially Western horses, are saddled and ridden while still quite young. Very often the young horse is taken out of the stall, has a heavy saddle thrown on his back, and then somebody is helped up whose main concern it is to stay on. There is no doubt in my mind that this is a traumatic experience for the horse. It is quite obvious that the pressure and the weight are painful because no muscles have been developed along the spine to cope with this sudden burden. In order to evade the pain, the horse tightens the muscles and a rigid back is the result. In the wild, or for that matter in pasture, one will see young unspoiled horses move with a totally decontracted body. Therefore, before putting any weight on a horse's back, first the back muscles must be developed by gymnastic exercises so that he can cope with a burden on his back. The simplest way to do this is by lungeing the horse (about which more later). Then, after a few months, gradually let the horse get used to having a weight on his back by putting a saddle on. Then lunge with the stirrups down. After a few weeks a person can hang over the saddle and a few days later can bring the right leg over to the other side and ease into the saddle, making himself as light as possible. While all this takes place, the horse should of course still be on the lunge line, the person who has regularly lunged the horse holding the line and making much of him. If, after all this, the horse still tightens his back when being ridden, one should repeat the exercises discussed above.

It is very important that a young horse learns to make correct changes of direction, because this is the way to teach him to use his back; an inexperienced rider can do a lot of harm to the horse by misusing the hands in the turns. The way to teach a totally untrained horse to change direction is to use the opening rein. The inside arm has to be stretched as far as possible to the inside, and the fingernails have to face upwards so that there is no downward pressure of the snaffle on the bars of the horse's jaw. In the beginning the outside hand should be totally passive. The action of the inside hand brings the head in, while the inside leg, with the toes up so that the calf muscle is hard, presses just behind the girth, thereby activating the inner hindleg. As soon as the horse has understood that he has to make a turn, the outside hand, a little higher than the inside, pushes the outside rein against, but never over the neck. When the outside hand goes over the neck, it will pull the head to the outside. That outside rein has to be taut enough so that it can function more or less like a stick. In this way the horse learns to move the shoulders inward on the pressure of the outside rein, the indirect rein.

When the horse does not need the help of the opening rein any more, then the time has come to teach him the correct way to make a change of direction, namely by bending round the rider's inside leg and by a slight flexing of the poll, caused by a light vibration of the rider's inside hand, so that the rider can just see the shimmer of the inside eye. A way to find out if the horse has understood the meaning of the indirect rein is to turn right, using the right opening rein, then to turn left with that same rein, now as indirect rein against the neck.

The inside rein has now to be used to get the horse to flex so that the rider can see the shimmer of the inside eye. Consequently, the horse will look in the direction he is going, and eventually he will yield to the rider's hand, by flexing the poll and letting go in the jaw.

The inside rein should be taut enough so that the vibration of the rider's hand can come through to the horse's mouth. Sometimes a gentle upward rotation of the hand is enough to get the flexion. The rider's hand should stay close to the withers, to prevent the head from coming in.

By supporting the horse with the outside rein, pressing it against the neck to ask for a change of direction, and using the inside rein only to see the shimmer of the eye, the rider will not impede the inner hindleg from making a large stride, which he would do if he pulled on that rein. The goal is to have the horse make a large stride with the inside hindleg because this effort will gymnastically develop the back muscles. Later we will discuss what the rider's legs are supposed to do during a change of direction.

The turn to the left is generally the most difficult. This is caused by the fact that most horses have a natural bend to the right side which causes the head to be carried slightly to the right. The result is that the horse takes the left rein and does not accept the right rein. There are several explanations for this phenomenon. I think that the most logical explanation is that there is no such a thing as symmetry in nature. Human beings are right and left handed; some horses take the right rein, most take the left. The result of this taking of the left rein is that, in a turn the horse will shorten the stride of the inner hindleg and will fall over the left shoulder. This should make it clear how important it is to get the horse to make a correct turn, because in this way he will be able to gymnasticise the back muscles. But how difficult this is! D'Auvergne (1729–98) wrote: "It is the never ending problem for every rider with every horse to get him to go evenly on both reins." What we ask the horse is as difficult as if we were asked to use our right and left hand in the same way.

There is a difference between the method and the goal. "Ideally the actions of the legs and the hands should be so discreet that the eye cannot catch them." (l'Hotte.) Before we can reach this goal we have to manipulate; we have to do things with the hands that are visible. This is the method. However, we should always bear in mind that the less we do, the better. Since the mouth of the horse is very sensitive, we should try never to hurt it. Hard, insensitive mouths are man-made.

In the walk the horse makes a snake-like movement from side to side; if this movement is allowed to go through to the hands, they will make a sawing movement, alternating left and right. Many horses go better when the rider carries the reins in one hand. For this reason, when riding with two hands, the rider should keep them so still and so close together that the horse has the impression that only one hand is holding the reins. The easiest way to achieve this is to put the nails and the knuckles of the thumbs together.

One has to consider what happens when the rider makes these sawing movements when he is using a curb bit. It is easy to understand that an unbroken bit makes much more movement in the horse's mouth than the snaffle when the rider has sawing hands. For this reason it is a very bad habit to carry the reins of an unbroken bit in two hands. How can the rider expect the horse to have confidence in his hands when this piece of solid metal is constantly moving in his mouth? Therefore, I believe that one should never carry the curb reins in two hands.

It is a kind of mental laziness in modern man to think that because it is easy, there is nothing wrong when one pulls right and left all the time. An example, mentioned previously, is the action of riding a bicycle when making turns.

When man first began to ride he had the reins in one hand, for the simple reason that he had only one hand available; with the other hand he carried his weapons, either for hunting or for fighting. For example, the Huns attacked without reins in their hands. They went at the enemy in waves, shooting one arrow when they were close enough; then they turned and while turning shot their second arrow; then while galloping away to make room for the next wave they shot their third arrow. To this day, the cowboy and the mounted bullfighter ride with one hand. The riders of the Spanish Riding School and a few classicists ride with a double bridle with the two curb reins in the left hand along with the left snaffle rein, and the right snaffle rein alone is in the right hand. From the basic position with hands level, the thumbs on a forty-five degree angle so that the back of the hands look like a slanting roof, the rider manipulates the reins while they are in one line: elbows, fists, mouth. When asking for a turn, the outside hand goes a little higher so that the rein presses against the neck. In transitions to a slower gait, it is often helpful to turn the nails of one hand up, and sometimes even the whole hand. The reason for this is that the snaffle, being a jointed bit, will act like a nutcracker when the rider resists with level hands, the horse's jaw will be pinched. This pinching of course hurts the horse and he will react most of the time by tossing his head up or by fighting the rider's hand.

Now I am going to focus my attention on the impulse-creating aids, the seat and the legs, which sometimes can also function as guiding aids. We have seen why it is important to have a correct position in order to apply the aids.

Unfortunately the wrong translation of a German expression has caused a lot of misconceptions about what one should do when one wants the horse to go forward, when one wants to create impulsion. The Germans use the expression "das Kreuz anziehen". This has been translated as "brace the backbone". As a result, people thought that the idea was to round the small of the back by collapsing in the abdomen and by being heavy in the saddle. This causes the knees to go up; consequently, the calves lose muscle tone, resulting in jiggling legs. The combination of the loose lower legs and the pulled-up heels causes the rider to poke his heels constantly into the horse's belly; it also causes the upper body to be all over the saddle and to interfere with the horse's balance, because the rider will not have a consistent centre of gravity.

"To brace" means "to fasten against, to increase tension". In this context "anziehen" means "to tighten". The backbone is the lower part of the spinal column; the small of the back is "das Kreuz". We have mentioned previously that when the muscles in the small of the back, as well as the abdominal muscles are tightened, the lordosis straightens. One can only straighten the small of the back when one makes oneself tall by using the abdominal muscles. The result of all this is that the pelvis tilts forward and upward, so that the backside of the seat-bones pushes into the saddle (this is why there should be two impressions in a privately used saddle): the tone of the calf muscles increases, causing the lower legs to lie still against the horse's belly.

It is evident that the stretching of the spine can only be done by the abdominal muscles and back muscles, which makes it clear that the rider not only uses these muscles for the guiding aids but also for the impulse-creating aids. When necessary, the driving of the seat can be strengthened by the closing of the calves. When the toes are pulled up, the calf muscles harden and a lot of pressure can be applied. Under the influence of Caprilli, the slogan became "talloni bassi", the heels down. The disadvantage of pushing the heels down is that the lower leg often goes too far forward. The correct placing of the lower leg is very important; it should lie just behind the girth. For the observer the stirrup leather should be perpendicular. When the rider wants to move the haunches to the outside, the pressure should be applied a little more back. The same procedure should be applied when the rider wants to prevent the horse from bringing the haunches in or out.

Earlier we discussed making a change of direction. The focus was then on the hands. Now we will concentrate on the function of the seat and the legs while making a turn. With the inside hand the rider places the horse's head so that he sees the shimmer of the inside eye, which allows the horse to look where he is going. With the outside rein the rider pushes the horse's shoulder in the direction he wants to go. When the rider indicates with his body, by rotating the spinal column, where he wants to go, he helps the action of the outside rein. We have seen already that the pelvis can be tilted forward and upward, but the pelvis can also be rotated. Looking with the head does not influence the rider's seat, but looking or turning with the hips and shoulders does influence the rider's seat and hands.

When the rider is sitting correctly square to axis, by easing the outside rein a little he prevents it from becoming too tight, and thereby holding back. When he rotates his pelvis, bringing his outside hip-bone forward, the pressure on the inside seat-bone increases. This pressure can be reinforced by pushing the inside knee deep. It is very important that when one pushes the knee down, the heel stays in the line: shoulder, seat-bone – heel. The goal is to bend the horse around the inside leg, which is impossible if the lower leg is too far back. (The inner leg too far back is a common mistake during shoulder-in, because it pushes the haunches out and brings the horse in the position of leg-yielding, which will be discussed later in some detail (Chapter 10).)

To reinforce the pressure of the calf the rider can use spurs. The spurs should be attached to the boots in such a way that it is not necessary to pull the heels up when using them. We have already explained why the heels should never be pulled up. If a horse is lazy it may be appropriate to apply the spurs. The application should be like one stinging attack, out of the knee, without displacing the knee. One sharp attack is better than a repetition of weak ones. A contemporary French author wrote: "The spurs should be sharp as daggers so that after one application the horse knows that he has to respect them." I do not go along with this method but it is something to think about when one sees all those riders constantly poking their spurs in the horse's belly while the horse could not care less, being totally dulled to them. The purpose of the spur is to wake the horse up and to emphasise the action of the calf.

The crop should be used with totally green horses who know nothing. A little tap on the shoulder accompanied with an encouraging voice command will get the horse to move forward. Gradually this has to be accompanied by the rider stretching his spine and the closing of his calves. Generally the stretching of the spine will increase the tone in the calf muscle, which can be enough. One has to be careful not to press constantly with the calf as some horses will tighten themselves up against legs that work like a vice.

For advanced schooling, the rider should use a so-called dressage whip, rigid and 120 cm long. It should be used just behind the calf as a substitute for the spur or calf in case the horse for some reason does not react properly to the leg aids.

The best way to use the whip is to bring the hand that carries it to the inside and then to rotate the wrist. A light tap will be the result. More is generally not necessary, and often the sound against the boot is enough. One should not forget that this is an encouraging, stimulating action. By bringing the hand in and rotating the wrist one avoids yanking on the horse's mouth, which is, of course, a counterproductive action.

It should be well understood that the whip is an aid, not an instrument to punish. All too often what is called disobedience is the result of bad schooling; the horse does not understand or is physically not yet able to do what the rider asks him to do.

The rider should realise that spurs, crops and all the different reining contraptions are not really aids. At the most, they should be considered to be means to reinforce and sometimes to replace the aids. (In a side-saddle the lady has to carry a whip on the right side because both her legs are on the left.) When carrying the reins three and one, the whip should always be carried in the hand that holds the one rein.

I cannot finish this chapter without mentioning the voice, which is an aid just as the others we have discussed. Article 417.4 of the F.E.I. dressage rules says: "The use of the voice in any way whatsoever, or clicking with the tongue once or repeatedly, is a serious fault, involving the deduction of at least two marks from those that would otherwise have been awarded for the movement when this occurred."

As a result of this rule a Swedish competitor in the Grand Prix, during the 1932 Olympic Games in Los Angeles, was put last because of allegedly clicking with the tongue, although he had high marks. This episode evidently so scared American dressage enthusiasts that nobody dared open his mouth. I remember my first involvement with an American Pony Club in the late 1950s. I was amazed that nobody ever spoke to his horse.

This was, of course, the result of a misconception. There is an immense difference between a pony clubber and a Grand Prix rider, and there is just as big a difference between a young or untrained horse and a horse with Grand Prix schooling. One should never forget that there is a difference between the method and the goal. The goal, of course, is a horse and rider combination that executes the most difficult movements without anybody hearing or seeing how the rider influences his horse. Part of the method to achieve this goal is to use the voice.

Federigo Grisone dedicated a chapter to the use of the voice in *Gli Ordini di Cavalcare*. And de Pluvinel wrote: "The voice is the spur of the mind." One of the great advantages of using the voice is that one can practically do no harm to the horse, which cannot be said about the other aids. Everybody who lunges knows how fast the horse learns the meaning of different sounds. Why not take advantage of this, and in the beginning of schooling under saddle get the horse to walk, trot and canter on voice command? The voice can have a calming effect on the horse. Therefore, I think that outside the dressage arena there should be a lot of talking. The words are not important, but the tone is. My advice is: first speak, then whisper, and finally think. This way nobody will hear you.

One can hardly call the clicking of the tongue a voice command, but it does encourage the horse. In eastern Europe the sound produced by the vibrating tongue is the command for a down transition. I learned this in München-Riem where I heard Ottokar Pohlman, an East Prussian, making this sound. When I later tried this with my Polish Trakehner, who had been in America for several years, I found to my amazement that the horse recognized the sound and responded to it.

Since we are living in an epoch in which mechanics and mechanisation reign supreme, some people seem to forget that the horse is a living being, which we should respect as such. There are members of the veterinary profession who disgrace it by forgetting that their first concern should be the well-being of the horse and not the ambition or pocketbook of the rider or owner. No veterinarian should act like the pit-crew at a motor-race. If the car has mechanical trouble, the driver pulls into the pits, the mechanics do their job, push the car back on the track and off the driver goes again. A real horseman knows his horse and feels what can be asked of him. Marit Kretschmar in *Pferd und Reiter im Orient* (1980) found that in at least two Turkish epics it was stressed that a commander who broke off a battle because the horses were too tired to go on was praised while two other people were frowned upon. Of these two, one, who had lost his son during a hunt, had kept his horse going during the night in searching for his son and the other had ridden three days and three nights to save his brother. The ethical relationship between man and horse was very strong with the Turks. Times have changed and man is not dependent on horses any more; but this does not mean that we should forget the supreme qualities of this extraordinary living being. The horse is by nature a gentle, non-aggressive animal, only too willing to co-operate, provided however that he is treated with gentleness and firmness. If you treat him as a motorcycle you are in for trouble. Jeanne Boisseau, in *Notes sur l'enseignement de Nuno Oliveira* (1979) quotes a maxim of Oliveira's: "If the horse is happy, everything will be all right; if he is constrained everything will go wrong. And in case that it is necessary to use force, then one enters a domain that does not fit the equestrian art, neither for that matter, in the circle in which civilised people dwell."

I end this chapter urging my readers that we apply the aids to help the horse, not to put him in a mould.

One should avoid resistances, instead of trying to conquer them

AUBERT

4 Lungeing

One of the practices where misconceptions are rampant is lungeing. There are two reasons for lungeing. One is to benefit the horse; the other is to benefit the rider. It benefits the horse because lungeing is a very important help to school, re-school and to take the edge off a horse that is frisky, possibly because he has not worked very much. As far as the rider is concerned, lungeing will help him find his balance on a moving horse, because the rider does not have to think of the horse and therefore can concentrate exclusively on himself. Lungeing also makes vaulting possible.

For both schooling and vaulting it is essential to have the proper equipment. First, a cavesson made of leather with reinforced noseband is necessary; under no circumstances should a nylon noseband be used. It is irresponsible to hitch the lunge line on to the bit, because we should at all costs avoid hurting the horse in the mouth. Xenophon wrote in *The Art of Horsemanship*: "The groom should also be instructed never to lead the horse on the rein which gives the horse a hard mouth on one side . . .". In an emergency one can use a halter, putting the line through the inside ring of the halter, bringing it over the nose, and then tying the line on to the outside ring. This works as a weak replica of the cavesson.

The lunge line should be about 10 m long, strong and supple and not more than 3 cm wide so that it is easy to handle. There should be no chain at the end of the line. At one end there should be a snap and on the other end a loop, wide enough so that in an emergency the lunger can slip his hand out of the loop. The lunge line should be fastened on to the middle ring of the cavesson. The lunger should take the loop in his outside hand. (When lungeing on the left hand, the lunger's right hand is the outside hand.) The line should not be wound around the hand, as the hand could be caught in the line if the horse runs off. Therefore, one should make a bundle of the line, laying it in the hand, by making figures of eight. The outside hand also carries the whip, while the inside hand guides the horse.

There should be a well-balanced lunge whip available, 2 m long,-

with a lash 30 cm longer. The whip should be used to encourage the horse to move, not by cracking it or by switching it, but by swinging the arm out of the shoulder, similar to casting, as the fisherman does with his fishing rod. After a lot of practise, it should be possible to throw the lash, by an arm movement, to a given spot on the horse's body. If the horse has the inclination to fall into the circle, the whip should be pointed at the shoulder. In case this does not work, one can try to throw the lash towards the horse's head or to make an upward movement with the hand holding the line so that the slack in the line goes to the horse's head.

Before one starts to lunge a young horse, one should realise that it is very important that an atmosphere of confidence exists between the lunger and the young animal. Establishing this atmosphere starts the moment the youngster is handled. There should be no teasing, no beating with whips, no scaring. When a young horse snaps (mainly colts will do this), give him a slap with your hand on his face and say, with much emphasis, "*No*", then pat him. Horses are very sensitive to being patted or stroked, and the voice is also very important. Once the horse has confidence in his master, he will respect and not fear him.

With a totally young horse, the lunger should begin by leading the horse through the arena, to get him acquainted with the surroundings. Then he should lead the horse in a circle, holding the horse close to the head. This can also be done by a helper. Where there is only one person to do the lungeing, he should generally move some distance from the horse, walking on the circle near the hindquarters; he points the whip behind the hindquarters, so that his right arm (holding the whip and the bundle of line) and the left arm (guiding the horse) are similar to the spokes of a wheel. As the horse begins to understand that he is supposed to move on a circle the lunger diminishes his own movements. In this way he becomes the hub of a wheel.

In a circle on the left hand, the lunger's left foot is the inner foot. He lifts it and puts it down on the same spot, similar to a horse doing a turn on the haunches. His outside foot, in this case the right, makes a small circle around the inside foot. This is very important, because the purpose of lungeing is to loosen and decontract the horse so that he will be able to use his back muscles. Therefore, it is necessary to bend the horse laterally, and this is only possible when the horse has to go around an axis, in other words, on a truly round circle. When the lunger keeps walking around, there is no more axis, and consequently no true circle.

The lunger should prevent the horse from leaning on the inside shoulder with his head to the outside. Right from the beginning the horse should learn to bend to the inside. Therefore, the lunger should constantly pull the head in with a gentle movement of the inside arm, bringing the fist towards his chest. This is not a hanging movement, but a give and take movement. The lunger should try to make the horse engage the hindlegs, either with his voice or with the whip. Once the horse has learned to stay on the circle, then the exercises should be done in a lively trot, leading to the working trot.

Is lungeing dangerous? Some veterinarians are strongly against it. One well-known rider claims that it can cause broken legs. My answer is a very categorical "No". Lungeing is not dangerous. In more than 40 years of experience, 20 in the Netherlands and 25 in America, I have never had a lame or injured horse because of lungeing. I have only twice used bandages or ankle boots and only because the owners insisted on it.

There is no better way for the initial schooling of the horse than lungeing. It is important that the horse learns to trot unimpeded by the weight of the rider. The daily routine during a three month period of lungeing should be for 20 minutes at the most. Lungeing should be mostly at the trot alternated with walk to rest and an occasional canter, to strengthen the back muscles and loosen the horse by eliminating contractions.

If the horse is full of energy and wants to canter or gallop at the start of a lesson, let him, so that he gets it out of his system. In this case the lunger should let the line be as long as possible and eventually he can move with the horse. Shortening the line and checking in a rough way can cause damage to the legs, and can break the spirit of the horse. When a horse falls into a trot after a short while, insist on a few more rounds in the canter.

If a horse learns the trick of running away over the outside shoulder, you are in trouble. Mostly he will try to do it in the same spot; in that case move to a side of the arena where he will find a wall. Sometimes it may be necessary to construct a barrier, so that the horse is enclosed.

For horses that tend to be on the forehand or are totally disconnected, I use side-reins with rubber rings: I also use them to let young horses get used to the bit. With horses that carry their heads too high I previously used draw-reins. Lately I have been using the Gogue.

My advice for the use of all these reins is: *be careful*. More horses have been ruined by misuse of these reins than I like to think of. If you decide to use them, begin by having them as long as possible and gradually shorten them. Do not try to collect a horse by tightening the side-reins, and do not try to force the head down by shortening the draw-reins or the Gogue. If you do, you are really asking for trouble. There is nothing a horse hates more than being constrained; he will either fight it or surrender and come into a faulty frame.

As a guide to the diameter of the lunge circle, it should be such that with the correct equipment the trainer is able to just touch the horse with the end of the lash when handling the whip in the proper manner.

In this chapter I have tried to describe how to go about lungeing, and the misconceptions and pitfalls one may encounter. A treatise about lungeing riders and about vaulting is outside the scope of this book.

The highest mark should be given when the influence of the rider is invisible. Because of the fact that many riders have a deficient seat, they try to compensate this by increasing the use of the hands and the legs

KURT ALBRECHT

5 The Confusion about the Working Walk

In 1977 the American Horse Show Association introduced the concept of the working walk into the dressage world. One may wonder why this bold innovative step was taken. In none of the other countries, many with a long tradition of dressage riding, has there ever been a question of the working walk. There are good reasons for this omission: in those countries the leading authorities recognised the fact that with young horses one has to be very careful not to ruin the walk by prematurely trying to establish a set, unelastic contact with the horse's mouth. The *German Cavalry Manual* (1912), discussing the working gaits, is very explicit: "As far as the walk is concerned, greatest attention should be given to the creation and maintenance of a correct and pure walk; therefore premature and strong resistance with the reins should be avoided. An incorrect, uneven and dragging walk will improve most of the time after the horse has learned to trot properly."

The rules governing the new movement were poorly written. They included a combination of sentences describing partly the medium walk and partly the working trot. The A.H.S.A. rule book (1982–83) describes the working walk as a "regular and unconstrained" walk. One wonders, why call this a working walk? The medium walk is described as a "free, regular and unconstrained" walk with moderate extension. According to the above description, the working walk should not be free, while the medium walk should be free and have a moderate extension. Seunig equates the free, regular and unconstrained walk with the walk for general use, sometimes called the ordinary walk.

In a working trot, the rider has to try to develop the engagement of the hindquarters. In order to do this, he has to keep the horse more or less together. In any case he has to prevent the horse from becoming too long, which means that there has to be some restraint with the reins. In the working walk, however, the horse should be encouraged to become long. In any dressage competition, one can see that most riders try to get their horses together when they have to execute a working walk. One cannot blame them, because that is what they have learned to do in the working trot. The walk must be developed differently from the trot for two reasons: (1) in the walk the horse always has one or more legs on the ground; (2) the footfall sequence being lateral, it can very easily become pacing if the rhythm is interfered with or constrained.

Basically the walk is therefore a gait of relaxation. The real work in the walk comes when collection and extension are asked for. These gaits, however, are far beyond training level. In the first year of schooling, the walk should be strictly a movement of rest between the short periods of trot. During those rest periods the walk should not be loitering, but the rider should forego the temptation to try to put the horse into position: that is, to try to elevate the forehand. The rider should have the horse on the long rein, which means featherlight, elastic contact, with the rider's hands following the movements of the horse's head. If the rider succumbs to the temptation to monkey with his hands, then there is a great chance that the horse will not accept the bit, will start tossing his head, will lose the push from his hindquarters and start pacing.

It is my conviction that the A.H.S.A. would show great leadership by abolishing the working walk, because it cannot be instrumental in improving the standard of dressage in America.

In 1983 the A.H.S.A. published new tests. In some of them the riders are asked to lengthen the stride in the walk, very likely analogous to the lengthening of the stride in the trot. However, the movements during the trot and the walk are incomparable. The striking difference is that the lateral movements of the walk do not have real impulsion. In order to keep the walk pure, the rider has to be very careful with his hands; whatever forward movement he is able to create with his driving aids should not be interfered with by the hands.

The trot is the gait to gymnasticise the horse because during it he has only two feet on the ground, alternated by a floating movement. Once the back muscles have been strengthened and, as a result, the horse has become able to use his back then the rider can begin to ask for collection. When the hindquarters come under and the hocks are flexing, then one can carefully begin to ask for a collected walk. After the horse has learned to collect during the walk, then one can begin to ask for lengthening and, eventually, for extension. The extended walk is a very difficult movement. It is not very often that one sees a correct extended walk, even in Grand Prix. Most of the time the riders allow their horses a "free walk on the long rein". This movement lacks the impetus that one should see in the extended walk. It is my belief that the reason for this poor showing in the extended walk is caused by the fact that most riders lack the knowledge of what aids to use for this movement. It has become an axiom that if one wants the horse to move and to lengthen the rider has to use his legs, but this is not always the case. One can use too much leg and then the horse does not respond. René Gogue, in *Problèmes Equestres* (1978), makes clear that the rotating of the pelvis in the rhythm of the walk, so that the seat-bone on the side of the forward moving hindleg comes forward, is the logical way to help the horse to develop the extended walk. According to Gogue this rotating of the pelvis is also the best way to develop the piaffe. This has nothing in common with the massaging of the back as advised by some authors. It is my personal experience that the suggestion of Gogue is effective.

The best bit is the one in wise hands

GENERAL L'HOTTE

6 The Free Walk

A serious observer who watches the free walk in the lower level dressage tests will come to the conclusion that it is not easy to find any consistency in the manner in which it is performed by the various entries. Some horses will loiter while doing the movement, looking left and right, on a totally loose rein; others will go more or less straight on a loose rein, but at the moment the rider starts to adjust the reins in preparation for the next movement, the horse starts to jog. Then there are riders who have their horses go pretty nicely, with moderate action from behind, but still no rein contact, because they think the horse has to be free. It can be too free, as I have twice experienced while judging, when nicely moving horses stopped on the diagonal to scratch their heads on a foreleg.

I think that the confusion is caused by the misinterpretation of the word "free" in the context of a dressage test. Free in this context does not mean a free horse. It does mean a free movement: a movement that is decontracted, because there are no tensions and there is no constraint.

Another reason for the confusion is the wording in the A.H.S.A. rule book (1982–83) Article 3–4e states: "The free walk is a pace of relaxation in which the horse is allowed complete freedom to lower and stretch out his head and neck. The hindfeet touch the ground clearly in front of the footprints of the forefeet . . ." This rule is in accordance with the F.E.I. rule, Article 403,4–4 with the exception that the F.E.I. does not ask that: "The hindfeet touch the ground clearly in front of the footprints of the forefeet." The only time that the F.E.I. asks for this is in the extended walk. This makes sense, because there are a lot of horses whose conformation makes it very difficult to fulfil this requirement of tracking up. For those horses a lot of schooling is required to get them to track up, and there is no chance that they will be able to do it during relaxation. I do not think that it is fair to ask, during a period of relaxation, that the horse perform a movement that is practically impossible to execute, because of his confirmation.

Since dressage competition first began, one of the difficulties has been to achieve unity in terminology. People from different countries with different doctrines were part of the committees that organised dressage. The old rule books never had very much to say about the walk. For a long time there was the ordinary walk, (French "pas ordinaire") and the strong or extended walk (French "pas allongé") and, of course, the collected walk (French "pas rassemblé"). In the *German Cavalry Manual* (1912) a collected walk is mentioned, and a free walk in which 125 strides per minute had to be made. This proves that this walk was purely for military marches; it was called free because the horse had to be unconstrained during this movement. Seunig equates this free walk with the medium or ordinary walk.

In 1936, the Grand Prix test to be ridden during the Olympic Games contained a movement called "Freier Schritt", or free walk. When one reads the test it becomes clear that this free walk could not be a gait of relaxation. The test reads in part: "At C, on the right hand, collected trot to B, at B free walk on the long rein, at F turn right, at K turn to the left in the collected walk with adjusted reins."

In contemporary terminology it would have said: "At B medium walk on a long rein, at K collected walk."

As I hope to show in the next chapter, it was in 1975 that a rational terminology was agreed upon.

There is a saying that the horse should enjoy himself in his work, otherwise neither the rider nor the horse would be able to give an elegant performance

PLUVINEL

7 The Working Trot

Since the trot is the most important gait as far as the gymnasticising of horses is concerned, rule book terminology has changed very much over the years in describing it.

All the misconceptions and fallacies surrounding the working trot are proof that it is one thing to translate a foreign term literally and quite another thing to understand its meaning.

The A.H.S.A. rule book (1982–3) describes the working trot as "a regular and unconstrained trot, in which a horse, not yet trained and ready for collected movements, shows himself properly balanced ...". My question is: how can a horse that is not yet trained show himself in proper balance? Since the working trot is a schooling movement, it cannot really be covered by a definition. It has to be made clear to the riders what the purpose of this schooling movement is; namely, to activate the hindquarters and to get the horse steadily on the bit. This is a process in which a horse learns to trot in a steady, balanced way. Horses in the wild walk long distances when they move from one grazing place to another. They will trot a little when they play, and they may even do a few steps of passage when they want to impress. When there is danger, they will gallop. Therefore, what we really have to do is to teach the horse to trot in a consistent way, not just to play. Since the trot is the most efficient movement for the gymnasticising of the horse (only two legs at the same time being on the ground), we have to begin to teach him this gait and work on it until we have a horse that, to quote Bourgelat, "trots with impulse, being decontracted and in balance".

When we have achieved this, then the time has arrived for the real schooling work: suppling exercises, lateral and longitudinal flexions, and all the more difficult movements.

In the more than 50 years that the F.E.I. has given guidance to dressage, a lot of thought has been put into the writing of the rules and tests. During that process different doctrines collided with each other. The result was, most of the time, compromise. However, when one peruses the successive rule books, an evolution is also noticeable.

The following short survey may help clarify many of the misunderstandings and the general confusion existing around the different kinds of trot. The data available are the texts of the F.E.I. Grand Prix de Dressage of 1928 (German); 1936 (German and French); 1948 (German and French); 1967 (German, French and English) and the rule books of the F.E.I. 1938 (German and French); 1950 (French and English); 1958 (French and English); 1963 (French and English); 1971 (French and English); 1975 (French and English); 1983 (French and English).

1928	abgekürzter Trab short trot			starker Trab extended trot
1936	abgekürzter Trab short trot	Mitteltrab ordinary trot		starker Trab extended trot
1948	versammelter Trab trot rassemblé collected trot	Arbeitstrab trot ordinaire ordinary trot		Mitteltrab trot allongé extended trot
1950	trot rassemblé collected trot	trot ordinaire ordinary trot		trot allongé extended trot
1958	same as 1950			
1963	versammelter Trab trot rassemblé collected trot	Mitteltrab trot moyen ordinary trot		starker Trab trot allongé extended trot
1967	same as 1963			
1971	same as 1963 and 1967			
1975	versammelter Trab trot rassemblé collected trot	Arbeitstrab trot de travail working trot	Mitteltrab trot moyen medium trot	starker Trab trot allongé extended trot
1982	same as 1975			

The F.E.I. rule books 1948 and 1950 give the same definition of the ordinary trot; we read under # 171 ed. 1950: "Ordinary trot (natural, as normally used in road work). This is a pace between the extended and the collected trot. The horse goes forward freely and straight, goes well off the hocks, softly into his bridle, with a balanced and free action. The steps should be as even as possible and the hindfeet should follow exactly in the tracks of the forefeet."

A very important note is added: "The ordinary trot must not be confused with the Mitteltrab (German), a trot with a more elevated and energetic action, with increased flexion of all joints, it is a brilliant trot, which the horse is taught."

The rule book of 1958 gives the same definition. However, it adds the following: "The degree of energy and impulsion displayed at the ordinary trot denotes clearly the degree of suppleness and balance of the horse." The 1950 note, of course, is omitted. Consequently, the French text of 1963 has replaced "trot ordinaire" with "trot moyen", and the French text of the Grand Prix now also uses "pas moyen" and "galop moyen". For their national tests the French now also use "trot moyen".

As the above survey makes clear, 1975 brought important changes: the working trot is introduced and the English version of the rule book abandons the term ordinary trot and replaces it with medium trot. So, twelve years after the concept of "trot ordinaire" was dropped from the French version of the rule book and replaced by "trot moyen", the English version accepted the new concept and used the term "medium trot".

The very lucid description Hermann Friedländer gives of the working trot, in *Chronicle of the Horse* (1970), makes it clear that the working trot is something different than the ordinary trot, described in 1950 as "natural, as normally used in road work". It indeed is called a working trot, because the horse has to work in order to be able to execute a rhythmic, balanced trot, using all his muscles, so that he finally will be able not only to perform the trot as normally used in road work, but also that he can be schooled in the whole scale of the different trots. Working trot is in the first place a schooling gait. Although the Germans have an equivalent for ordinary trot, "Gebrauchstrab", they do not ask for it in dressage tests. Seunig sees the "Gebrauchstrab", a trot for practical use, as the end result of working trot, medium trot and a shortened trot. He emphasises that collected, medium and extended trot are pure dressage gaits. Dressage riding has a very broad foundation in Germany and, because of the still strong influence of the former military riding, there is one school of thought with which every German who starts riding is confronted. All are as familiar with these terms as with the alphabet, while foreigners are not.

In deciding what terms to use it, of course, makes a lot of sense to follow the F.E.I. terminology; it is up to the instructors and the riders to become familiar with the meaning of all these concepts by seriously studying them.

It is too, up to the judges to stress in their commentary the importance of the engagement of the hindquarters. Without this engagement there will be no balanced rhythmic trot; there will be no pure gait.

When, due to his conformation, one can only expect a limited extension from a horse, one should, if the movement is correct and rhythmic, evaluate this performance as high as the impressive lengthening of a horse that was born with this talent

KURT ALBRECHT

8 Lengthening of the Stride and Extending the Trot

Since the basic principles and common misconceptions about lengthening of the stride and extending the trot are the same, the problems can be dealt with in one chapter.

The old masters did not know an extended trot. Their concern was only to get the haunches under the horse, because originally in man-to-man battle the forehand had to come off the ground. This later developed into the school jumps, although it did not prevent these horses from going very well cross-country, after a little schooling. This is illustrated in a story told by Gaspar de Saunier (1756). Louis XIV, preparing to go on a campaign during one of his many wars, ordered that 40 horses be chosen from the stables in Versailles. They were Turkish, Berber and Spanish horses which had been exclusively schooled to do the school jumps. For the coming campaign they had to be prepared to go over rough country and to jump ditches. The beginning was very difficult; they stumbled, sometimes fell on their knees, and had difficulties keeping themselves up. They refused to jump, and even refused to go near ditches. The riders dismounted and tied a rope to the cavesson. This rope was held by a man on the other side of the ditch (in the way Xenophon had already described). When they finally had learned to jump the ditches while mounted, they proved themselves better than the best hunters, not only because of their speed, but also because of their stability on their legs in all sorts of country and also jumping ditches and hedges.

As far as I know, La Guérinière was the first to mention something that implies lengthening. He writes about a lively trot in which the horse lengthens himself ("hardi et étendu") in order to loosen the shoulders and the hindquarters. He advises using this trot when there is trouble teaching the shoulder-in.

After the French Revolution, there developed in Europe an interest in the English Thoroughbred and the way the English rode in the field. As a result, we find in the literature the beginning of the description of the strong trot (French "grand trot", German "starker Trab"). For example Hünersdorf (1800) writes about the lengthening of the stride ("ausgedehnter Trab"). He claims that the advantage of this movement is that the horse learns how to lengthen himself, is strengthened by these exercises, and is taught to go forward with head and neck correctly placed.

The Comte d'Aure (1852) wrote that speed is not obtained by allowing the horse to go forward in an impetuous way. The fact that d'Aure asks a group of riders to execute the lengthened trot ("trot allongé") on a circle proves that the length of this trot was far less than the length of the modern extended trot. Nowadays, the extended trot is not being asked on the circle, because it is impossible. Rather, it is the medium trot that now is asked on the circle.

Von Oeynhausen (1852) stresses that the trot be pure, which means that the diagonal feet are lifted and put down at the same moment. He wants the movement lively and diligent.

Faverot de Kerbrech (1891), interpreter of Baucher, writes that the strong trot ("grand trot") should be progressively developed out of the ordinary trot ("petit trot"). The movement should be free and resolute; the head should be close to the perpendicular, and the horse should go energetically and straight forward.

When reading these quotations, one has to remember that the authors lived during an era when the basics of equitation were still the engaging of the hindquarters and gymnasticising of the back. It is my opinion that the F.E.I. was stimulated by Caprilli to ask for extending movements in the dressage tests in order to get the riders out of the habit of pulling their horses together. I think that a misconceived interpretation of Caprilli is at the root of bad extensions. Caprilli wanted the horse unconstrained in going cross-country, so that the neck and back could be used. Unconstrained does not mean that the horse should go without any contact with the rider's hand, resulting in a disconnected horse. It does mean that the rider has an elastic contact with always straight reins "never" loops and with the tension varying from featherlight to firm. The

Illustration Plates

PLATE 1
The author competing in Rome, 1937

PLATE 2
A more leisurely pace at home in Cavendish, New England, 1979

3

PLATE 3
Sigmund von Josipovich

PLATE 4
Egon von Neindorff on Jaguar

Geza von Haszlinszky, of the Spanish Riding School, demonstrates piaffer

. . . and passage

PLATE 7
A pupil of von Neindorff; impeccable position

PLATE 8
Rider leaning backwards. A sight one sees only too often, even at the highest level of competition

6

PLATE 9
Stretching elbows

PLATE 10
Hands "playing the piano" resulting in the elbows being too far from the body and preventing a supple elbow movement

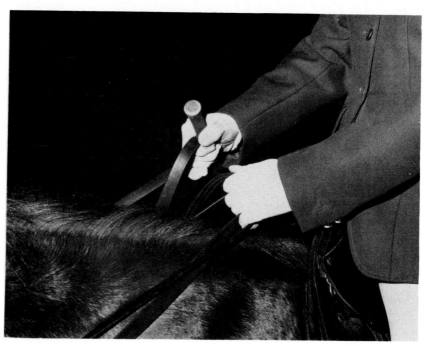

PLATE 11
Hands carrying the reins "three-and-one"

PLATE 12
A gentle upward rotation of the inside hand to see the inside eye. Inside rein close to the neck; outside rein against the neck, while vibrating the inside rein in order to see the shimmer of the inside eye

PLATE 13
Applying opening rein

PLATE 14
Hollow back

PLATE 17
A drawing reproduced from a frame of a film of Egon von Neindorff's stallion Jaguar. This horse covers as much ground as possible, he lengthens his steps to the utmost as a result of great impulsion from the hindquarters. According to von Neindorff he can bring his hindlegs far under, because his head is being kept perpendicular

OPPOSITE PAGE

PLATE 15 (top)
A horse that is on the forehand while the hindquarters are too high. The reason for this is very likely that the horse cannot bring the hindquarters under because of anatomical shortcomings. He cannot flex his hocks adequately, therefore the croup goes up and the shoulders down

PLATE 16 (below)
A drawing done from a picture of a horse being ridden by Waldemar Seunig. This is an example of the idea that the nose should come slightly forward. Because the nose is forward, one gets the impression of the horse becoming long in the frame, with the risk of falling apart

PLATE 18
The rider is preventing the horse from looking to the outside. The elbow is stretched so that the forward movement is not impeded

PLATE 19
The elbow is broken and the forward movement is impeded

PLATE 20
Here the rider has the knee too deep and sits on top of the saddle

PLATE 21
Bracing the backbone

horse does not object to firm contact as long as it is elastic; the horse resents and often fights a dead hand, one that is set or is pulling. With this elastic contact, the rider is able to keep the horse in balance.

When either a lengthening of the stride or an extension is asked for in dressage competitions, one sees only too frequently that the rider lets go, losing all contact. The result is that the horse falls apart and loses his balance, because the hindlegs do not push any more and they spread far apart. To some it may give the impression of a lengthened frame, but it is a functionally incorrect lengthening, because the hindlegs do not push, the back is not engaged; as a result the horse loses his balance resulting in rushing or coming on the forehand. A sure way to find out if the horse lengthens in a functionally correct way is to ask him to trot over cavalletti or to jump a low obstacle out of the trot. Most mistakes of allowing the horse to "fall into two pieces" can be corrected once the rider understands what lengthening of the stride and extension really mean. A far more serious mistake is to allow the horse to throw his front legs in the air and let them not only touch the ground later than the diagonal hindleg, but also bring the front feet back. In other words, the front foot is not touching the ground on the spot at which the foot, in its highest elevation, pointed. This is a difficult mistake to correct, because it is a movement that quite a few horses offer. To the layman it looks elegant, and the public thinks it is spectacular. For that reason, the judges may tend to overlook it. This movement is the result of a stiff back in the horse, and that is where the correction should begin.

According to the F.E.I. rule book (Article 404, 4.4) in the extended trot: "The horse covers as much ground as possible. Maintaining the same cadence (rhythm), he lengthens his steps to the utmost as a result of great impulsion from the hindquarters. The rider allows the horse, remaining on the bit, without leaning on it, to lengthen his frame and to gain ground. The forefeet should touch the ground on the spot towards which they are pointing." It has to be emphasised that it is the lengthening of the steps that should be the main concern. That is what the judges have to look at. The lengthening of the frame is secondary, because it is the result of the lengthening of the steps.

73

It is a misconception that in the extended trot the horse should put his nose forward. The aforementioned rule does not speak of either the nose or the head. The misconception is caused by the fact that for the extended canter the rule book mentions: ". . . the tip of the nose pointing more or less forward."

In this connection it is interesting that Faverot de Kerbrech wrote that the head should be close to perpendicular. In the *German Cavalry Manual* (1912) I find a picture of a horse in the extended trot with his head nearly perpendicular. The misconception that the nose be allowed to come forward may well be the reason that so many horses lose their balance or "fall in two pieces", which is worse. According to Egon von Neindorff, with whom I had a discussion about this subject several years ago, the horse loses the maximum forward drive of the hindlegs if the rider allows the nose to come forward. And this maximum forward drive is what the rules ask for: ". . . he lengthens his steps to the utmost as a result of great impulsion from the hindquarters."

A special problem is encountered with some of the European Warmblood horses. When asked to perform an extended trot they show something that is very spectacular: they float over the ground and barely seem to touch it because they show very distinct suspension. Sometimes it looks like an extended passage. It is a way of going the horse offers, not the result of schooling. At every stallion show in Europe, when they are shown in hand, one can see this way of movement. It is, of course, difficult to penalise something so spectacular, but I think we should, because this way of going is functionally incorrect.

It seems to me that rule 404 of the F.E.I. causes confusion by saying: "The trot is a pace of two time on alternate diagonals (. . .) separated by a moment of suspension." This can be, and is frequently interpreted, as if cadence, a prolonged suspension was being asked for. For this reason it might be better not to talk about suspension but a floating movement. I do not think that the trot is pure when the movement is not continuous. To suspend means, in a broad sense, to stop temporarily, to cause to cease or to bring to a stop.

This momentary stopping is what happens in the piaffe and in the passage, this is also the trot the Hackney is famous for. I do not

74

think that a trot with a moment of holding back is the trot for a riding horse.

It should be stressed that, when asking for the extended trot, the rider should never lean backwards. It is not only awful to watch from an aesthetic viewpoint, it is also functionally incorrect. It is also a misconception to think that the rider has to put his weight backwards in order to engage the hindquarters. The rider's centre of gravity behind the plumbline prevents the horse from swinging his hindlegs well forward. At all times the rider has to be with the movement of the horse and not behind it. The trouble is, of course, that most of the great champions do lean back, and what champions do is imitated by those less fortunate.

In a dressage competition the focus is on the performance of the rider–horse combination, the unity of this combination and the willingness and the ability of the horse to respond to the rider's indications; in breed classes, the extravagance of the movements may be a point of consideration.

To recapitulate: in either the lengthening of the stride or in the extended trot, the rider should drive to create impulsion in the movement of the horse, and he should maintain the contact with the horse's mouth in order to prevent the horse from losing his balance. In the extended trot he should also be sure to prevent the nose from coming forward in order to get the maximum push from the hindquarters.

Finally I would like to quote part of F.E.I. rule book, Chapter II, Article 420, 4: "The test includes all the school paces and all the fundamental airs of the Classical High School, of which the fancy (author translation) paces, based on extreme extension of the forelegs are no part . . ."

Nothing good can be achieved without tempo and rhythm

CESARE FIASCHI

9 Tempo, Rhythm, Cadence

Since I believe that there is a lot of confusion about the exact meaning of "tempo", "rhythm" and "cadence" I want in this chapter to try to define them.

All three terms are used in music, dance and verse. However, one does not find always clear-cut definitions for them in dictionaries. Very often, rhythm and cadence are considered to be virtually the same, and also are quite often regarded as interchangeable. The following definitions are, therefore, applicable to equitation only.

Tempo is the speed over a certain distance. For example: in the military, the tempo for the walk was 100 m per minute; for the trot 200 m per minute; for the canter 350 m per minute. The rules for combined training specify the tempo for the steeplechase to be 690 m per minute. When the horse is asked to extend, he is supposed to cover more ground; that is what is called the increasing of the tempo. The horse should not increase the frequency of the movement, or, as the F.E.I. rule book says (Article 404.4) should be "maintaining the same rhythm". (Changed in 1983 to cadence.)

Rhythm is a fluent sequence of movements in a certain beat. When a horse misses a beat or when the length of the strides becomes uneven, the horse loses rhythm.

Instead of giving cadence almost the same meaning as rhythm, I suggest using this term in reference to movements of prolonged suspension, such as piaffe and passage. The F.E.I. rule book says in Articles 413 and 414 that these movements should be "very cadenced" or "highly cadenced" and with "prolonged suspension". Lately, one sees more and more that in the extended trot the front legs are thrown out with some suspension. This cadence in the extended trot may be spectacular, but it is against the rules and it is functionally incorrect. The purpose of the lengthening of the stride, and eventually of achieving an extended trot, is to show that the horse is able to lengthen and shorten his frame. This, of course, is what makes the horse more versatile. I would like to see a horse in a "cadenced extended trot" go at an obstacle.

Riders should form a clear idea about these expressions, because, in the schooling of a horse and eventually in riding a test, they should be able to maintain an even tempo, rhythm and, in passage and piaffe, cadence. Often in lower tests, one sees that horses sometimes go faster, sometimes slower. This is seen especially after a turn; for example, from B across the arena to E. The horses go faster because they fall apart.

In the trot, especially, the rhythm should be lively and well accentuated. The sequence of the movements should be continuous. When there are moments of prolonged suspension (for example the trot of the Hackney), then the trot is cadenced.

When the horse does not engage the hindquarters, has a stiff back, or when the movement is dull, then there is no lively and accentuated rhythm. The rhythm is also lost when the beat is uneven. This can, of course, be caused by uneven footing; it generally is, however, the result of the fact that the horse does not carry himself.

Cadence, as I interpret it, is only asked for in the piaffe and in the passage. Because of the prolonged suspension, the sequence of the rhythmic movements is not continuous. That makes the difference with the pure trot. What pure trot and passage and piaffe have in common is that they all three should be rhythmic. A piaffe in which the movements are continuous is not correct, because there is no prolonged suspension. One sees this faulty piaffe only too often, especially when the rider in desperation makes more movements than the horse.

To conclude: even tempo, rhythm and cadence can only be achieved by a horse that engages the hindquarters, carries himself and is permeable.

A righteous man regards the life of his beast; but the tender mercies of the wicked are cruel

10 Leg-yielding

There is a lot of confusion regarding the exercises shoulder-in and leg-yielding. This confusion has been stimulated by a statement, made by an influential teacher, that when the test asks for a shoulder-in and the horse executes a correct leg-yielding, he would consider the movement to be sufficient.

I hope to make it clear that shoulder-in and leg-yielding are two totally different exercises. Leg-yielding supples or loosens the hindquarters, but brings the horse on the forehand. Shoulder-in supples or loosens the shoulders and engages the inner hindleg. It was because of the limited effect that leg-yielding had on the overall suppling of the horse, that la Guérinière looked for a better way and as a result of his reflections invented shoulder-in.

According to the old Masters, leg-yielding has a lot of drawbacks. For example Waldemar Seunig in *Am Pusschlag der Reikunst* (1961) had this to say about leg-yielding: "Leg-yielding's purpose is preparation for two track work. The advantage in preparing two track work, just as well attainable by other less dangerous exercises, is generally outweighed by these disadvantages:

A) Because the horse is being ridden on a slightly wider track without bending, full development of vigorous use of the hindlegs is hampered and a loss of pure gait is very possible even with sensitive riders.

B) The hindlegs do not support enough because they are not yet able to tread under and therefore move outside of, the track of the front legs instead of forward in the direction of the centre of gravity. The horse, stumbling sideways instead of moving forward and sideways, loses poise and rhythm and falls on the shoulder.

C) The fact that the forehand does not precede the haunches during the sideways movement gives rise to the danger that, while stepping over, the inside front leg will hit the outside front leg, causing spavins."

Under the influence of Seunig's book, leg-yielding was dropped from the dressage tests in 1964, and soon afterward the turn on the forehand out of the standstill was also dropped.

Long before Seunig, Louis Seeger wrote in his book, *System der Reitkunst* (1844), that the shoulder-in is the best exercise to teach a horse to be obedient to the leg, to yield to the leg. What nowadays is called leg-yielding Seeger refers to as "head-in, haunches out". He is against this movement because it brings the horse on the forehand, and since the legs have to cross each other they are in each other's way, thus hindering the movement. Seeger, like Seunig, warns about the risks of lameness resulting from this movement. Such risks include shoulder lameness, which can be caused when the shoulder is pulled forcibly inwards and sometimes forward in direct antagonism to the pectoral muscles; bowed tendons caused by strain on the ligaments and tendon sheaths of the front legs; stepping on the coronet band caused by the crossing action of the front legs, and thickness of the knees caused by straining of the bursa of the tendon surrounding the knee-joint.

Gustav Steinbrecht in *Das Gymnasium des Pferdes* (1884) wrote: "Two track movement without bending and collection are always wrong exercises." He also warns about the lameness Seeger was concerned about and he includes splints, which can also be caused by strain on the surrounding ligaments or trauma to the splint-bone area. Notwithstanding these warnings of the old Masters, leg-yielding has been reintroduced as a schooling movement, and institutionalised as a test movement.

Oberbereiter von Niedermayer (1837–1887), quoted by Podhajsky, stated that head-in, hindquarters-out, could only have been invented by human want of judgement. Applied unreasonably and without moderation, this exercise is damaging for every horse (Niedermayer). Podhajsky in *Die Klassische Reitkunst* (1965) states emphatically that the turn on the forehand and leg-yielding do not belong in classical exercises; they can never be more than expedient. For this reason, they should never be asked for in a dressage test, not even for beginners.

Nobody contests that the horse should be obedient to the leg and eventually yield to the leg. But this loosening exercise should never be done on the straightaway. The reason that leg-yielding on the circle is beneficial is because the horse does not lose impulsion, the centrifugal force taking care of this. What on the straight line becomes a stumbling movement becomes on the circle a rhythmical movement in which the inner hindleg can swing well over the outer hindleg, while on the straight the swing can only be moderate. Therefore it is only on the circle that leg-yielding becomes a real suppling exercise for the hindquarters. To quote Podhajsky about leg-yielding: "On the circle and only for basic schooling."

On the straight line and on the diagonal the inside leg is limited in how far it can step over. I have the impression that this is the reason why those who practise leg-yielding excessively on the diagonal generally make very poor half-passes.

It is incomprehensible to me that anybody could have thought up such a movement as leg-yielding on the diagonal which has a disastrous effect on the half-pass, this is the leaning on the shoulder, in the direction of travel. Later, in the half-pass, this is the gravest mistake because the horse then has to be bent and look in the direction he is going.

To execute leg-yielding on the circle, one should tighten the outside rein, the hand a little up and press the rein against the neck in order to push the shoulders in on the circle. In this way the shoulders of the horse are stabilised so that they can function as a kind of mobile pivot around which the haunches can turn. If the rider tries to get the horse on the circle by using the inside rein, he will stop the forward movement if he applies the direct rein of opposition (pulls), he will destabilise the shoulders if he applies the opening rein, pulling the head in. The taut outside rein will cause a slight bend. The inside leg presses well behind the girth. In the beginning, after two sideways movements of the horse's hindquarters, one should go straight with little tension in the reins, making the horse go well forward. After a few strides straight forward, one asks for yielding to the other leg. In case the horse has difficulties understanding what he is supposed to do, a helper should use his fist in the place where the rider's leg is supposed to act. This exercise should be limited to the beginning of the schooling period, until the horse is able to make half-circles stepping well over. The circles are on two tracks.

By tightening the outside rein and pressing this rein well against the neck, a half turn on the forehand can be developed. If one insists on making turns on the forehand, this is a better way than first letting the horse come to a halt, allowing it to lose impulsion, and then trying to make this turn with a lot of pounding with the heels. While the latter may be a pragmatic procedure, it is certainly not an equitational one.

The rider who asks for leg-yielding should be well aware of the fact that the sole purpose of this exercise is the suppling of the hindquarters. He should try to avoid combining this exercise with any other exercise, because it will totally confuse the horse.

A last word of caution: the horse can only engage the hindlegs if they move on a straight line. When the inner hindleg steps over the outer hindleg, the hindquarters swing out. When the inner hindleg steps in front of the outer hindleg, the hindquarters can still stay on a straight line. When the hindquarters swing out, they cannot push any more and the movement becomes defective. I am convinced that a lot of the poor movements one sees all too often are the result of an overevaluating of the need to practise leg-yielding.

It is not the speed, neither the number of strides, that should be evaluated during the pirouette, but it is the rhythm of the jumps and the maintenance of the balance during the turns

HANS VON HEYDEBRECK

1 The Turn on the Haunches and the Pirouette

Since the turn on the haunches leads to the pirouette, the execution of both these movements reveals the same basic shortcomings most of the time. For this reason, it is possible to discuss both these movements in the same chapter. The difference between the two movements, according to the rule book, is that in the pirouette the inner hindfoot should come down in the same spot, or slightly in front; in the turn on the haunches, the inner hindfoot is not required to come down in the same spot but may move slightly forward.

The very important requisite of both movements is that the inner hindleg should make distinct steps, and the inner hindfoot should not stick to the ground (pivoting). Very often one sees this pivoting on the inner hindfoot and, maybe more often, pivoting on the outside hindfoot, when the horse shifts his weight to the outside.

I am convinced that faulty execution of these movements is the result of wrong methods of teaching. In the first place, one has to realise that the horse has to be engaged for both movements. In order to make sure that the horse will keep stepping with the inner hindleg and that he will lift that hindfoot off the ground, without veering to the outside because of shifting his weight, it is important to begin teaching these movements on the circle. The circle should be about 8 m wide, and the horse should be placed in the travers (haunches-in) position. Great attention must be paid to the movement of the inner hindleg and that the horse keeps the weight on the inside and does not shift to the outside. When the horse has learned to do this, then the circle should become gradually smaller in diameter. The emphasis all the time should be on the stepping of the inner hindleg, and one should be sure that the hindlegs do not fall out of the circle. The French call this "les deux bouts en dedans", "moving with both ends in". Gradually the circle becomes so small that one can speak of a turn on the haunches, and finally it will become a pirouette.

Especially in the canter pirouette one has to take great care that impulsion is maintained. Very often one sees the rider slow down just before asking for the pirouette. If this slowing down is not accompanied by an increase in the driving aids, it is impossible to execute a correct pirouette, because the horse will have lost collection.

According to the rule book, the turn on the haunches can be executed from a halt or from a walk, while the turn on the forehand should be executed from the halt. There is a danger in asking for both these turns from a halt. Most horses lose their engagement when they come to a halt, and one must remember that none of these turns can correctly be executed by a horse without proper engagement.

Those who devote themselves to practice without science are like sailors who put to sea without rudder or compass and who can never be certain where they are going. Practice must always be founded on sound theory

LEONARDO

Pignatelli, convinced by his own experience that the function of the bit is rather to let the horse know what the rider wants than to constrain the horse, said that if the bits had of their own the miraculous quality to make the mouth of the horse and to make the horse obedient, both rider and horse would be all set after a visit to the tack shop

LA GUÉRINIÈRE

2 La Guérinière and Shoulder-in

The controversies around shoulder-in will very likely never end. Therefore, I think it might be a good idea to go back to the source and find out what de la Guérinière really said.

In 1733 François Robichon de la Guérinière published a book called *École de Cavalerie*. This authoritative work is considered to be the standard of Classical Equitation. Unfortunately, a genius on horseback is not necessarily a master of language. In his use of language, de la Guérinière was not very disciplined and this provoked misconceptions and caused Parocel, his illustrator, to draw the wrong diagrams.

To understand the aim of de la Guérinière when he conceived the idea of shoulder-in, one should read very carefully what he said in explaining how the concept of this movement developed. In the beginning of the chapter he states that trotting on the straight line results in only limited suppleness, as it helps the forward movement of the shoulders and the legs. The difficulty starts he says, when we try to supple the horse so that he can make circles and sideways (lateral) movements.

Salomon de la Broue, a contemporary of de Pluvinel, and the Duke of Newcastle both had theories on how to achieve this suppleness, de la Broue making some use of circles and also of what we now call cavalletti.

As we shall see shortly, the Duke of Newcastle was a great influence on de la Guérinière but, surprisingly perhaps, de Pluvinel was not. One may wonder why in *École de Cavalerie* there is no reference to de Pluvinel. It seems that la Guérinière did not think too much of de Pluvinel. He mentions him once, in the opening paragraph of the chapter on the pillars: "The pillars are an invention of M. de Pluvinel, who had the honor of putting Louis XIII on horseback. He has left us a treatise on riding. The prints it contains are valued by the curious because of the quality of the engraving and by the fact that they show how the gentlemen of the court of Louis XIII were dressed."

The Duke of Newcastle's theories were to greatly influence la Guérinière when he developed the shoulder-in movement. This can be seen in *École de Cavalerie*, where de la Guérinière frequently quotes the Duke of Newcastle and then adds his own comments. Several examples are included here.

"The head-in, the haunches out, on the circle, brings the horse on the forehand . . . The shoulder cannot become supple if the inner hindleg does not come close to and in front of the outer hindleg." Following these quotations la Guérinière says: "This admission, which experience confirms, makes it very clear that the circle is not the true means to supple the shoulder . . . a profound truth that this illustrious author admits is that the shoulders can only be suppled when the inner hindleg comes close to and in front of the outer hindleg; it is this judicious remark that has put me on the way to find the exercise shoulder-in."

Now follow two quotations from de la Guérinière himself about the advantages of shoulder-in (bracketed words I have added to aid comprehension). "This exercise supples the shoulders because the inner foreleg moving forward, crossing over the outer foreleg, and the inner (hind) foot moving in front of the outer (hind) foot, coming down in the line of that foot, causes the shoulder to make a movement that activates the joints of this part of the horse's anatomy." Later he adds:

"Shoulder-in prepares the horse to bring more weight on the haunches, because during every stride he makes in this position he brings the inner hindleg forward under the mass and puts it in front of the outside hindleg, which he cannot do without dropping the inside hip . . . thus he learns to flex his hocks." A little further on one reads: "The line of the haunches close to the wall, the shoulders about one and a half to two feet from the wall."

By contradicting himself repeatedly in *École de Cavalerie*, de la Guérinière has created confusion about the movements of the legs and about the question of how much the shoulders should go off the tracks. In the edition published in 1751, on page 107, he first quotes the Duke of Newcastle, when he says that the shoulder cannot be suppled unless the inner hindleg moving forward comes close to the outer hindleg; then Guérinière says that the inner front leg crosses and moves forward over the outer front leg ("croiser et chevaler *par* dessus"), and in the same way the inner hindleg over ("*par* dessus") the outer hindleg. In connection with this sentence, he refers to the diagrams (showing very definitely the stepping over): then, when he enumerates the advantages of the movement shoulder-in, he states: "In the first place this lecture supples the shoulders, because the inner foreleg crossing and moving forward over ('*par* dessus') the outside foreleg and the inner hindleg moving in front of ('*au* dessus') the outside hindleg and on the line of that same foot; the movement the shoulders have to make, activates the movement of the joints. In the second place: 'Shoulder-in prepares a horse to put more weight on the hindquarters because during every stride he brings the inner hindleg under his belly and puts that leg in front ("*au* dessus") of the outer hindleg, which causes a flexion of the inner hock.'"

One gets this picture: the haunches go straight along the wall, with the inner hindfoot in front of the outer. The inner hindfoot should not cross over the outer, because this causes the haunches to swing out, becoming leg-yielding (see Chapter Ten). The shoulders are brought in, not the head, because, as the Duke of Newcastle had to admit, this brings the horse on the forehand. The inner foreleg crosses the outer foreleg, the rider sees the shimmer of the horse's eye (flexion), the horse is bent around the inside leg of the rider, and the horse is not looking in the direction he is going. The hindquarters propel because they move straight.

Of course, one can only begin to ask the horse for shoulder-in after he has become obedient to the leg, and one should realise that one can only gradually get the horse to correctly execute shoulder-in. The Germans speak first of shoulder-fore, with which they begin the schooling. In it, the print of the inner hindfoot is between the prints of both front feet. As the horse becomes more supple, the shoulders will be able to come more in, because the horse will be able to bend and the print of the inner hindfoot will cover the print of the outside front foot.

Before asking for shoulder-in, the rider should prepare his horse by putting him in position, seeing the shimmer of the inside eye by giving gentle indications with the inside rein; the inside leg should be closed, just behind the girth. (If the leg is too far back, the horse cannot bend around the leg.) The outside leg is passive but ready to prevent the haunches from swinging out (causing leg-yielding). The outside rein, held in a hand a little higher than the inside pushes the shoulders gently to the inside of the track. The hand should never go over the neck. In case the horse brings the shoulders too far in, then the inside hand pushes them back.

When de la Guérinière was trying to find a way to loosen the shoulders and hit on the concept of shoulder-in, he got as a bonus something he was not looking for, the flexion of the hocks. Thus shoulder-in not only became a loosening exercise, but also a collecting exercise. Shoulder-in is the pre-eminent exercise to get the horse to flex the hocks, without which no real collection is possible.

It is, of course, questionable if shoulder-in and for that matter leg-yielding are really movements for a test. As late as 1971 the rule book of the F.E.I., Article 411, 5a said: "The shoulder-in is a movement (usually) not required in competition or exhibitions but a schooling exercise, developing the obedience of the horse and the skill of the rider, at the same time being the foundation of lateral movements." It is only in the rule book of 1975 that both leg-yielding and shoulder-in were promoted to test movements.

To conclude, it is my conviction that we find the correct description of the shoulder-in by analysing the genesis of this movement, as de la Guérinière describes it and by attaching considerable importance to his statement about why he considers shoulder-in so important. Evidently Gustave le Bon, the French psychologist, in the fourth edition of his book *L'Equitation Actuelle et ses Principes* (1913), was also struck by the contradictions. He marked: "The fact that the riding masters find difficulties to formulate their methods and contradict themselves can often be explained by the fact that when they ride they use unconsciously their nervous system and when they write they consciously use their nervous system."

Postscript

The F.E.I. ended the controversy in 1983, after the above study had been written, by publishing a new rule Article 411.7.2 in which most of the wording of the third paragraph in la Guérinière's chapter on shoulder-in is used.

The violence which accompanies athletics deprives mankind of its intellectual qualities, qualities to which he owes it that he is a man. . . . the pagan worship of the muscle goes directly against what until our days had been the vocation of humanity, that is the passion for comprehension, for intelligence

SOBÈNE OLSTEF

13 Reflections

To end, I would like to reflect upon the state of competitive dressage in its relationship to classical equitation. In order to do this, we have to come to grips with a few basic problems. In the first place, what really is dressage? I think that it is a big word that puts a lot of people off; on the other hand, quite a few people who participate in dressage competition feel themselves far above the crowd.

Instead of "dressage", I would rather use the phrase "schooling the horse", because that is what we really should do when we prepare a horse for the level we want to compete in. The purpose of competition is to find out how far we have advanced in our attempt to prepare a horse for a certain level.

Whatever our ultimate goal may be, eventing, show-jumping, classical dressage or even driving, we have to realise that the basic goal is to help the horse find its balance. He can only find his balance when he engages his hindquarters, uses his back and becomes supple. In every dressage ride we should see that the horse is engaging (not dragging the hindlegs); we should see that the horse is able to execute the lateral and longitudinal flexions for the level in which he is being presented. The horse should be carrying himself, he should be permeable and he should also be obedient.

When we keep all requisites in mind and then think back upon what we have lately seen, live, on television, or on film, it is not a very rosy picture that comes to mind. To keep the record straight, sometimes there are some surprisingly good exceptions. But only seldom do we see a working trot where the hindquarters are engaged.

In the lengthening of the stride or in the extensions, the horse usually loses his balance and falls in two pieces. The transitions are generally too abrupt and lack longitudinal flexion. The turn on the haunches and pirouettes are generally poor, as a result of a lack of lateral flexion and a loss of impulsion. The shoulder-in is most of the time non-existent, because the rider evidently has no clear conception of what the horse is supposed to do during this movement.

At the national level, it is mainly due to poor instruction that the performances are disappointing. It is of course a great privilege to live in a democracy where everybody can say what he wants to. However, as far as equitation is concerned, it would be better if there were more discipline and more humbleness among those teachers with little experience and even less theoretical knowledge.

The basic problem for dressage in America is its youth and consequently it has no doctrine. In Europe there are also difficulties with the coming and going of innovators. But there are always national doctrines to fall back on, when the new theories outlive themselves. The F.E.I. has its troubles; the ground rules are impeccably classical, but the rules that go into details do not always follow the classical concepts.

It was not long after dressage started to expand in America that many Europeans came as instructors. The trouble with this is that they all had different national doctrines. In order to give the reader an idea of what was going on in Europe during the last hundred years, a short history of dressage may be useful here.

Until the Second World War, dressage riding in Europe was mostly influenced by the requirements of military riding. Many of the guiding ideas found their origins in the teachings of de la Guérinière, especially in Germany and in the Austro-Hungarian Monarchy. In France, as a result of the revolution, dressage had a difficult time finding the way back to its classical foundation as developed by the school of Versailles.

In the second half of the 19th century, the French equestrian world was ripped apart by the followers of Antoine d'Aure and François Baucher. The first was a pupil of one of the d'Abzac brothers, who had been "écuyer ordinaire" in Versailles. Although d'Aure developed into a cross-country rider, he never forgot what d'Abzac had taught him. Baucher spent his youth in Milan, Italy, where he became a pupil of Mazzuchelli, a then well-known riding master. Supposedly under the influence of his teacher Baucher developed his famous – for some people infamous – thesis that the will of the horse should be destroyed and the horse should be totally subdued to the will of the rider. He wanted to destroy the instinctive forces, while d'Aure wanted to use these forces. This different approach points to a cultural schism; there are those who love and those who dominate. Regarding horses, there are "dresseurs", (trainers – in this context people who school) and "dompteurs" (tamers). There is no doubt that Baucher has enriched the hippological vocabulary. He invented the flying change every stride and he taught his horses to canter on three legs and to canter backwards. In Vienna, where Baucher gave performances, he was called the gravedigger of French equitation. Through the influence of the Duke of Orléans, a son of Louis-Philippe, King of France, who was at that time president of the cavalry commission, Baucher was called to Saumur, the military riding school. But when the duke was killed in an accident shortly after, his brother, the Duke of Nemours took over the presidency of the commission and not being an admirer of Baucher, Baucher was asked to leave. Some time later d'Aure was named "écuyer en chef" at Saumur. Ever since, Baucher's ideas have had varying influence.

Baucher's influence was at its lowest in the 1930s when General Decarpentry was president of the dressage commission of the F.E.I. In this function, he came in close contact with General von Holzing-Bersted, the President of the F.E.I., also with Gustav Rau and Ernst Lindenbauer, one of the great Oberbereiter of the Spanish Riding School. It looked then as if the whole of equestrian Europe had adopted one doctrine, inspired by de la Guérinière. It did not last long. After the Second World War, France, presumably out of chauvinistic reasons, turned back to Baucher. The Swedes, who used to be followers of the classical German school turned to Baucher, very likely under the influence of Major St. Cyr, twice Olympic Gold Medal winner, who had been on detachment in Saumur.

The classical German school with such names as Steinbrecht, von Heidebreck, Lörke, Burkner and Rau, to name a few, has given way to what I call the neo-German school. In contrast to the classical German school, this one is purely competition oriented. From my point of view, Reiner Klimke is the personification of the neo-German school. Michel Henriquet told me in this connection a revealing story. When Henriquet visited Klimke in Münster, they discussed classical dressage. At the end of their conversation,

Klimke said to Henriquet: "You are very likely right, but I ride dressage competition every weekend and I want to win." Furthermore, the commentator in *Reiter Revue* of October 1982 had this to say: "The acknowledgement of his phenomenal achievement as a rider does not take away the notion to see in the pair Klimke–Ahlerich from a hippological standpoint a problematic and also a controversial winning combination. As far as his skill in the saddle is considered the new champion is a master without peers, he fails however when one considers the schooling of the horse by means of gymnasticising exercises in order to achieve: pure gaits, a horse without constraints and with collection as the principle goal." To this I want to add that although Klimke was during the Olympic Championships in Los Angeles without any doubt the winner, his presentation, in my opinion, lacked brilliance and did not reach the high standards of classical dressage. Reiner Klimke is a very intelligent and industrious man. Helped by his instinct he has found the weaknesses of the system, which has helped him to reach his goal – winning.

The influence of the Austro–Hungarian school is still traceable today, though since the end of the Second World War we cannot speak of a living Hungarian school any more. After the First World War, the Austro–Hungarian Monarchy was split up. In Vienna the Austrian school lived on, thanks to the Spanish Riding School; in Hungary the traditions of Vienna were continued until the Second World War. From the defunct Austro–Hungarian school there have been very important remnants with influence to this day. For example, Sigmund von Josipovich (1869–1945), instructor at "das Kaiserliche und Königliche Reitlehrer Institut" (school for future military riding instructors) in Vienna until 1914. After the First World War, Josipovich became chief instructor at the Hungarian military riding school, first in Budapest, then Orkeny-Tabor. Geza von Haszlinszky (1900–80) was an instructor there. One of his pupils was the man who later should create the American show-jumping style, Bertalan de Nemethy. After having been an instructor at Orkeny-Tabor, he became commander of the Spanish Riding School in Budapest. He was taken prisoner of war by the Russians during the Second World War and sent to Siberia. After his release, the Hungarian communist government made him a csikos (herdsman for horses). Due to the intervention of Prince Bernhard of the Netherlands, then President of the F.E.I., he was set free and allowed to go to the Netherlands. He spent the rest of his life in a position at the Dutch court. Waldemar Seunig and Alois Podhajshy were pupils of Oberbereiter Gottlieb Polak, during their stay at the Spanish Riding School. Furthermore it could be said a number of Germans belong to the Austro–Hungarian school because of their education; Richard Wätjen, who worked twelve years at the Spanish Riding School, Fritz Stecken and Egon von Neindorff, both pupils of Ludwig Zeiner, Bereiter of The Spanish Riding School. Neindorff also worked with Wätjen.

The neo-Germans and the Swedes have the greatest influence as far as dressage riding is concerned in America. However, there are still a few adherents of the classical German and Austro–Hungarian school around. From what I see happening in America, it is evident that a mix of all these different doctrines does not work. The cultural epoch we are living in is not favourable for classical equitation, of which beauty is a fundamental aspect. Modern man is more interested in things mechanical, in acrobatics. But there are still many people who are interested in art for the sake of art, who yearn for what is beautiful. I only partly agree with Egon von Neindorff who said that the adherents of classical dressage are an endangered species. Nothing in history is static; therefore I believe that classical dressage one day will make a comeback. In this context, it was very encouraging to read the reservations expressed in *Reiter Revue, Information Hippique* and *Plaisirs Equestres* in connection with the outcome of the 1982 World Championships in Lausanne.

As far as the international standard is concerned, it seems to me that the inadequacy of many judges, and the complexity of the tests, are to blame for the poor standard of the so-called Grand-dressage. In order to evaluate the standard of international dressage riding in a justifiable way, we have to accept an equitable standard: the standard recognised by the F.E.I. In Chapter I, Article 401, Object and General principles, we read:

Paragraph 1: "The object of Dressage is the harmonious development of the physique and ability of the horse. As a result it makes the horse *calm*, supple, loose and flexible, but also confident, attentive and keen, thus achieving *perfect understanding with his rider.*"

Paragraph 2: "These qualities are revealed by: (1) the freedom and regularity of the paces; (2) the harmony, lightness and ease of the movements; (3) the lightness of the forehand and the engagement of the hindquarters, *originating in a lively impulsion*; (4) the acceptance of the bridle, with light bit contact ('submission throughout' is a wrong translation of 'decontraction totale') and without any tenseness or resistance."

Paragraph 3: "The horse thus gives the impression of doing of his own accord what is required of him. Confident and attentive he submits generously to the control of his rider, remaining absolutely straight in any movements on straight lines and bending accordingly when moving on curved lines."

It is worthwhile pondering these lines and asking ourselves how often have we seen a horse in competition, even at the highest level, who was calm, supple, loose and flexible, with lively impulsion and in understanding with his rider? Or a horse that accepted the bit without tenseness or resistance? How often have we seen movements obtained without apparent effort of the rider as required in Article 417? In the final mark to be given in the Grand Prix test during the 1948 Olympics in London, not only the position and seat of the rider, but also the discretion of the aids applied by the rider had to be evaluated.

Since 1969, having twice visited Wolfsburg, twice Aachen and Goodwood and gone to the Olympic dressage championships in Bromont, Moscow and Los Angeles, and having read the comments about the big meetings by the experts in English, French and German magazines, I cannot say that, measured by the standards given in the F.E.I. rules, what has been presented was very good. Often I have the impression of a downward trend. It seems to me that the main reason for this poor showing lies in the difficulties of the tests. There was a time when one spoke about classical or academic equitation: what we see now looks more like acrobatic equitation. One gets the impression that those who put these tests together do not try to compose a coherent whole, with artistic value. It looks as if they have the preconception that difficulties have to be created, in the same way that the builder of a show-jumping course purposely creates difficulties. The present F.E.I. dressage tests consist of some very difficult movements, strung together one way or another, leaving little room for the grace, beauty and charm that correct dressage should exhibit.

The old Masters tried to create beauty and they knew that they could only achieve this by having a horse that was *really permeable* (durchlässig). As people close to the Renaissance, they pursued the Greek ideal of "kalos k'agathos" (what is beautiful and what is correct). They did not dream of competing with each other by riding a prescribed set of movements within a certain time limit.

I realise that we are living in a time in which there has to be competition. But would it not be possible to have competitions with the emphasis on beauty and not on acrobatics? With the emphasis on acrobatics there is too much tenseness in both horse and rider. Therefore, the performance cannot be brilliant and there cannot be continuous permeability. The acrobat in the circus or in gymnastic competition alternates his tours de force, his stunts, with relaxing movements. In the test for the Grand Prix, all the difficult movements have to be executed one right after another without any decontracting movements.

Maybe it would be a good idea to get a choreographer to help with the composition of the tests. This could spare us the boredom of the present tests and maybe it would help to conserve the brilliance that dressage horses are supposed to show.

Article 418 says: "The F.E.I. instituted an International Dressage Event in 1929 in order to protect the Equestrian Art from the abuses to which it can be exposed and to preserve it in the purity of its principles, so that it could be handed on intact to generations of riders to come." This article is very important because it not only uses the term equestrian art, thereby making art the kingpin around which dressage turns, but it also requires those in charge of the F.E.I. to preserve the art in its purity of its principles.

In this book I have, hopefully, explained what causes the loss of the artistic elements in, and the mechanisation of, the performances, namely the composition of the tests. The present tests are concatenations of very difficult movements, making it impossible for any horse and rider combination to perform equestrian art. The composers of the F.E.I. tests should remember that the rules want to protect the art and they should realise that the art can only be protected if the tests have rhythm so that the horse and rider combination can produce an artistic performance. As it is now the performances can only be mechanised.

For the judges, who have to concentrate on all those difficult movements which follow each other like machine-gun fire, it is very difficult to really assess the rider and even more difficult to get an impression of the whole. As a result there are judges who claim that only the performance of the horse should be judged. They evidently have never read Article 417, which says: "All the movements should be obtained without the apparent effort of the rider", and a little further on ". . . enabling the rider to follow the movements of the horse smoothly and freely . . ." In this context it should also be remembered that Article 401.3 says: "The horse thus gives the impression of doing of his own accord what is required of him."

There is another ticklish point to which my attention was drawn. In 1893 W. J. Gordon wrote a book called *The Horse World Of London*. I found therein an interesting concept which I quote: "The ease with which a man will lose his eye for a horse is notorious. Let even a good judge live for awhile among second-class horses and he will insensibly modify his ideal; and he will only get back to his true taste by another stay in first-class company." It seems to me that this is also applicable to dressage judges. I wonder if any of the present-day judges have ever been exposed to real equestrian art, when the horse gave the impression of doing all the movements of his own accord and when "the use of the rider's hands and legs were so secret that the eye could not catch them" (l'Hotte, *Questions Équestres*).

Ideally, a well-composed test has two components: one, the technical execution of the movements where the judges have to evaluate the functional correctness; two, the judge has to ask himself, "Was it artistic?" The evaluation of the functional correctness is, for a judge who knows what he should be looking for, an objective judgement, while the artistic is a purely subjective one.

In evaluating the rider's position, his influence on the horse and the application of the aids, the above-mentioned components are more or less interwoven. A rider who sits incorrectly and is rough can never be elegant. The judge fails if he takes into account the fact that the rider is able to keep the horse under control. He should evaluate how he influences the horse. A horse that has to be kept under control in order to prevent trouble does not belong in the dressage arena, certainly not at the Grand Prix level. At this level a horse should be perfectly obedient. This is the main purpose for the schooling of the horse.

The F.E.I. should get serious about "preserving the principles of the equestrian art" by having tests composed in which the horse and rider combination can display art. Furthermore the F.E.I. has to find a way to formulate a doctrine based on Articles 401, 417 and 419 in order to give the judges a standard. It is evident that the present format of the judge's forum does not work. It should be impossible that statements are made such as: "When the test asks for a shoulder-in and the rider performs leg-yielding, that the mark should be at least sufficient." Another comment: "In the piaffe it is not necessary that the hindlegs come under." There should be an equitable way to take the judges card away from those who flout the rules, either because they do not know the rules or because they think that they know better. The same procedure should be applied to judges who do not have enough self-discipline to set limits to their subjectivity and wander away from what they are actually supposed to judge.

This is no easy charge, considering the cultural epoch in which we are living, where there is no time for reflection, where everything has to go fast, where there exists a certain awe for things mechanical, where there is little respect for tradition and a certain aversion to discipline. Cultural phenomena come and go in waves. So there may come again a time when people will get bored with acrobatic equitation and turn back to artistic equitation. This is noticeable in other fields; for example, the upsurge of interest in the musical kur. For this reason we have to be grateful to the Article 419 which emphasises the protection and preservation of equestrian art. We should keep in mind what Charles Prosper, Chevalier le Vaillant de Saint Denis, "Écuyer cavalcadour de la grande écurie du Roi" had to say in 1789: "One must agree that if the true principles of the art had not been maintained, with a certain austerity in the royal riding school in Versailles, if they had not been constantly practised, someday one might be hard pressed to find the ways to renew the principle."

Glossary

A.H.S.A.	American Horse Show Association.
F.E.I.	Federation Equestre International (International Equestrian Federation).
Ecuyer en Chef	First Rider and Director of the former military Riding School in Saumur, France.
Ecuyer cavalcadour	See Index Nominum, Versailles.
Ecuyer ordinaire	See Index Nominum, Versailles.
Gymnastic	Pertaining to physical exercises that develop strength and agility.
Gymnastics	The practice or art of gymnastic exercises.
Gymnastically	Adverb of above.
Exercises, loosening	To loosen or supple the muscles.
Exercises, collecting	To stimulate the flexing of the muscles.
Exercises, gymnastic	To develop the tone and strength of the muscles.
Tone	That state of the body or of an organ in which all its functions are performed with healthy vigour.
Gymnasticise	To make a horse perform those exercises that will enhance the horse to function with healthy vigour.
Manipulate	To work skilfully with the hands.
Martial Arts	Any fighting discipline, including all systems of combat.
Pankration	Oldest known form of Martial Arts, first mentioned in Greece, around 500 B C.
Kung Fu	Originated in China, one of the main founders of Kung Fu is said to have been Bodhidharma, a monk, who also originated Zen Buddhism in China. Kung Fu fighting involves many circular movements as well as using the fighting movements of the tiger, crane, monkey, snake and dragon.
Karate	Originated in Okinawa and Japan. Karate fighting involves many angular and straight movements.

T'ai Chi

Originated in China, roughly translated it means "Grand Ultimate Way". T'ai Chi fighting is yielding.

Permeable

The literal translation of the German expression "Durchlässig", meaning "letting through". A horse is permeable when it lets the impulsion, created by the driving aids of the rider, go from the hindquarters through the back and the neck muscles, causing flexion of the poll and causing the horse to accept the bit, without stiffening of the jaw. The acceptance of the bit means that the driving aids and the guiding aids have met. At this point the process reverses itself, the guiding aids regulating the impulsion, taking care of the longitudinal and lateral flexions and also of the different gaits and movements.

Index Nominum

Academy

According to Lilly Powell-Froisard, *Plaisirs Équestres* #121, we have to trace the origins of the Academies during the flourishing of the Renaissance in Italy. The Greek ideal of education, the body in harmony with the mind, received new life through the rediscovery of the Greek classics. All over Italy, Academies for young noblemen were set up. The curriculum included: Greek, Latin, painting, music, mathematics, astronomy, dance, fencing and equitation.

Evidently people like Grisone, Fiaschi, Pignatelli, Pluvinel and others had to set up these elaborate schools in order to get pupils. Or maybe some of them were just members of the staff.

Alexander Technique

Mathias Alexander was born in Tasmania in 1869; he died in 1955. His ambition was to become a singer and reciter; in the process he lost his voice. Not getting any help from the medical profession, he tried to find out for himself what was wrong. Looking in a mirror he saw that he tightened muscles around his throat. Out of this insight, Alexander developed a technique whereby a person can develop a good posture and gain complete control over his body, without becoming rigid.

Auvergne, Jacques, Amable d' (1729–98)

He entered the military service in 1744, with the "chevauxlegérs de la maison du roi". His first instructor was François de Lubersac, "écuyer cavalcadour" in 1736 and "écuyer ordinaire" in 1740. In 1750, Drummond de Melfort joined the chevauxlegérs. Lubersac was pure School of Versailles, while Drummond de Melfort was educated on the battlefields. It is there that he learned that the school movements taught at Versailles had no place in military riding. The cruel confirmation of his conviction was the outcome of the battle of Rossbach where, in 1757, the French cavalry was routed by the Prussians, under Seydlitz. In 1756, at 27, d'Auvergne was called to be the "écuyer en chef" of the École Militaire in Paris. (One of his pupils there was Napoleon.) D'Auvergne never published any books. However, some of his pupils, Bohan, Boisdeffre and de Chabannes quoted d'Auvergne extensively in their writings. For example, he objected to collected gaits, the balance on the hindquarters, and he stressed forward movements in a horizontal balance.

Baucher, François (1796–1873)

Born in Versailles, Baucher was sent, when he was 14, to his uncle in Milan, who was equerry to Prince Borghese, husband of Napoleon's sister, Pauline. From his later writings, it is evident that he came strongly under the influence of Mazzuchelli. In 1816, Baucher went back to France to work in riding schools in le Havre and Rouen. In 1834, he went to Paris to run a riding school with J. Ch. Pellier. In 1837, he joined the circus of Laurent and Adolphe Franconi. He did this to be able to show his interpretation of riding as laid down in his first book, *Dictionnaire raisonné d'Équitation* (1833). In that age, the circus was the gathering point for society. Baucher introduced himself as a renovator and claimed that before him nobody had ever really understood the essence of equitation. He showed: halt on three legs, trot backwards, change of lead every other stride, pirouettes in the canter on three legs, canter backwards. His performance caused quite a bit of commotion. His admirers consisted of The Duke of Orléans, Lord Seymour, Lamartine, Delacroix and Théophile Gauthier, while his antagonists counted among them the Duke de Nemours, Alexandre Dumas, George Sand and Gustave Flaubert. It is quite interesting to note that the world of letters took such a keen interest in what happened in a circus. In 1842 Baucher's main book, *Méthode d'Équitation*, was first published. It has become known as the "first method". Faverot de Kerbrech revised the text and added to it in 1874. This is known as the "second method". The aim of dressage as expounded in the first method is to break the will of the horse and to shape it into a docile instrument of the rider. Much was done standing still, severe bits were used and sharp spurs were not spared. In 1855 Baucher had a crippling accident when a heavy chandelier fell on him. This accident and the mellowing that comes with age brought the second method, in which the horse is schooled in motion. Less stress is put on the spurs and the advantage of the snaffle is put forward.

Bourgelat, Claude (1712–79)

He was born in Lyon, France and was educated by the Jesuits. For a quarter of a century he managed the Riding Academy of Lyon. There is a story that he studied law in Toulouse and practiced law in Grenoble. He also may have served in the cavalry, in a troop of the King's Musqueteers. In 1740 he was called to manage the Riding Academy. In 1744 he published his first and only book on equitation *Le Nouveau Newcastle, ou Nouveau Traité de cavalerie géometrique, théorique et pratique*. This was later to be followed by many publications on veterinary subjects. For many years, books have been written dealing with veterinary science and equitation. Originally, the emphasis was on the veterinary part, but later the emphasis shifted to the equitational part; in Bourgelat's case the change went to the veterinary. In 1762 he founded the first Veterinary School at Lyon. At the request of Louis XV, he founded the second Veterinary School at Alfort, just outside Paris.

Duarte, King of Portugal (1401–38)

He became king in 1433 but died in 1438, a victim of the plague. There exists a manuscript of his dated 1434 of which the title is: "The book to teach to ride well in all saddles". In the Iberian Peninsula, as a result of the Moorish occupation, during about six centuries, the Iberians had to adapt themselves to the ways the Moors fought in order to fight them successfully. The Moors rode a lighter horse, fast and manoeuvrable, against which the heavy western European horses had no chance. The Iberians also, after they had started to use the light type horses, adapted to the way the Moors rode and used short stirrups, with a high saddle. This was called riding *a la gineta*. This makes it clear that the Iberians had to be able to ride in two saddles. The manuscript of Duarte's book, for some reason, was found in the National Library in Paris. In 1842 the first Portugese edition was published in Paris and the second one in 1843 in Lisbon. There exists a fragmentary translation into French by Bacharach, published in *L'Année Hippique*, 1959. There is not a trace of cruelty in Duarte's writings; he evidently was a real *dresseur* and not a *domptuer*. Monteilhet, in *Les Maîtres de l'Oeuvre équestre*, ranks him between Xenophon and Pluvinel.

Fiaschi, Césare, (15(?)–75)

When Griso had his school in Naples, Fiaschi had his in Ferrara, probably about 1539. He wrote a book in 1556, dealing with subjects such as: "How to handle and how to bit horses and how to shoe them". This last part is considered to be excellent, while the other parts rank even with Griso's theories. Fiaschi introduced music during riding, because he believed that without music and rhythm nothing good can happen.

Glahn, Erich (1879–1960)

Glahn was a staunch defender of the purity of the principles of classical equitation. He was a frequent contributor to *Sankt Georg* and wrote *Die Reitkunst am Scheideweg* and *Die Weltreiterei und Wir*, as well as a few novels. Seunig considers him to be the successor of von Heydebreck and von Josipovich as advocate of classical equitation.

Grisone, Federigo (16th century)

His book, *Gli Ordini di Cavalcare*, was published in 1555. Grisone was a pupil of Colas Pagano, the son of the "écuyer en chef" of the King of Naples, D. Ferranto, the illegitimate son of the King of Aragon. This could mean that there was Spanish influence in Pagano's teaching. Since *Gli Ordini di Cavalcare* was the first book on riding ever to be published in Italian, it found a wide audience. It was translated into French in 1559 and into German in 1570. As happens so often, the bad things make more impression than the good things. And there certainly are a lot of bad things in this book. But after studying it carefully, it remains in one's memory as a mixture of great kindness and ruthless brutality.

A French critic had this to say: "He has, as many modern riders, sensed the theory, without knowing the theory." The same critic calls him a rider without peer.

von Heydebreck, Hans (1866–1935)

He was an acknowledged expert in equitation and wrote several books and aricles. Co-author of the German cavalry manual of 1912. Commentator of Steinbrecht's *Gymnasium des Pferdes*.

l'Hotte, Alexis Francois (1825–1905)

Friend and pupil of both Baucher and d'Aure (1798–1863). D'Aure was a pupil of the School of Versailles after the Restoration. He believed in a forward moving horse and strongly attacked Baucher. L'Hotte was able to bring the two opposed methods into a synthesis, proscribing, however, the extravagances of Baucher. He was in Saumur as "Écuyer" (1860–64), "Écuyer en chef" (1864–70), and as a general commanding officer of the whole of Saumur (1874–79). He wrote two famous books, *Questions Équestres* and *Officier de Cavalerie*.

von Josipovich, Sigmund (1945)

He worked together with von Heydebreck and was Instructor at K.U.K. Militär Reitlehrer Institut in Vienna. He had great influence on the development of classical equitation in Austria and Hungary.

La Broue, Salomon de (c. 1530–c. 1610)

A pupil of Pignatelli, he wrote the first book on riding in the French language (1593). His second book, *Le Cavalerice français*, which appeared in 1610, had a great impact. He differed from de Pluvinel in that he emphasised work in the exterior; he introduced what we now call cavalletti. He is also the first to ask for flexion in the poll. He stresses lightness: "The lightness of the mouth of the horse precedes the lightness of the horse." After he came back from Italy, he was for some time "écuyer ordinaire de la Grande Écurie du roi", to Henri IV.

La Guérinière, François Robichon de (1688–1751)

He was born in Essay, a small town near Alençon, where his father was a lawyer; he also was an officer at the court of the Duchess of Orléans. In 1715, he received his title as "écuyer du roi", which entitled him to give lessons. He never had a function at the palace in Versailles. He was a pupil of Antoine de Vendeuil, who at one time was "écuyer ordinaire" in Versailles. In 1730, Prince Charles of Lorraine, "grand écuyer de France" (master of the horse) named him director of the Manége at the Tuileries. Notwithstanding the fact that his reputation as an extraordinary teacher had become international and that he received pupils from all over Europe, he was most of the time in financial trouble. Evidently La Guérinière was not a good businessman. In 1731, he published his book, *École de cavalerie*. In contrast to most of his predecessors, La Guérinière was evidently a very methodical man. While La Broue, Pluvinel and the Duke of Newcastle ramble along and are very repetitious, la Guérinière has a strict scheme and stays with it. (Maybe it was because his father was a lawyer.) What contributed mostly to La Guérinière's fame was the fact that he invented the shoulder-in.

Newcastle, William Cavendish, Duke of (1592–1676)

William Cavendish was a man of great wealth; his grandfather had been Treasurer both to Henri VIII and Edward VI. He was a staunch supporter of Charles I in his fights with the Scots and with the Long Parlement. He helped the king out with £10,000 to raise an army, the treasury being empty and the king without an army. Later he raised an army for himself to help the king fight the Long Parlement. As a reward, he was allowed to mint money and to confer knighthood. At Marston Moor, however, he was defeated in 1644 and had to flee England. Via Rotterdam he arrived in Paris where he married a young lady in waiting to Queen Henriette and went from there to Antwerp, where he found lodging with the widow of Rubens, the famous painter. He started a riding school in Antwerp and operated it for 18 years. He wrote his first book in Antwerp, and he had the good fortune to find an excellent engraver, a former pupil of Rubens, to illustrate the book, Abraham van Diepenbeke, a Dutch painter, born *c.* 1607 in Bois-le-Duc. Originally a glazier, he gave this up because of the fire hazards. A prolific producer, he was very much in demand by book publishers to make vignettes and illustrations. In 1660, with the restoration of Charles II, the Duke went back to England. He retired from public life and lived alternately on his estates Welbeck and Bolsover. At this time, he wrote a second book. In a preface, he makes it clear that this second book is not a translation of the first (this one having been published in French) neither an expansion, but a new book because of new insights. After a bad translation into French by somebody who did not know anything about horses, Jacques de Solleysel, "écuyer de la Grande Écurie", made an excellent translation.

The illustrations in the book are beautiful, the text is very repetitious, the contents are controversial, and the Duke is an extremely vain man: according to him his method has never been thought of before; his ways are marvellous and nobody ever thought of them before; the authors who wrote before him did not understand anything about equitation. But he was an extremely faithful servant to his king.

Pignatelli, Giambattista (16th century)

Very likely born around 1525, he died presumably before the end of the century. He was a pupil of Fiaschi. There are no writings left of Pignatelli (however, there should be some manuscripts of him around somewhere). Pignatelli was a rider and teacher of great fame and he has had an everlasting influence on the development of equitation in Europe. Four of his most distinguished pupils were Salomon de la Broue (1552–1602), Antoine de Pluvinel (1555–1620), de St. Antoine, whom Henri II sent to Queen Elizabeth, and George Engelhard Löhneysen Della Cavalleria (1588) who brought equitation to Germany.

Pluvinel, Antoine de (1555–1620)

At age ten, he was sent to Italy where he studied under Pignatelli. At the riding academies in those years the pupils received a complete education. Back in France, he was attached to the court of the brother of King Charles IX, the Duke of Anjou. In 1573, this duke was elected King of Poland, and Pluvinel accompanied him to his new kingdom. When, in 1574, his brother Charles IX died, the Duke decided to give up the throne of Poland and to go back to France. He fled from Poland with three French noblemen, one of which was Pluvinel; they rode non-stop from Cracow to Paris. In 1589 Henri IV succeeded to the throne of France at the death of Henry III. Pluvinel kept all his charges under the new king: chamberlain, tutor of the dauphin (later Louis XIII) and of the Duke of Vendome. In 1594 Pluvinel was licensed to open a riding academy in Paris. It seems that as a young man, the Cardinal de Richelieu was a pupil at Pluvinel's academy. In 1609 he was sent as ambassador to the Netherlands, where he met Crispyn de Pas, Jr. who was an engraver in Utrecht. Thanks to this meeting we have the most beautiful engravings of any book on horses. I think that de Pluvinel's fame was mostly due to these engravings. Pluvinel took notes, on the orders of the king, whenever he gave lessons to the king (Louis XIII had been his pupil when he still was dauphin). Pluvinel had given those notes to his friend Menou de Charnizay to safeguard them, hoping that later he would be able to use them in order to make a book. However, Pluvinel died before he had even started to order the notes. Crispyn de Pas, who had practically finished the etchings, got hold of a friend of his, a servant of Pluvinel, by the name of Peyrol, who managed to get him a collection of discarded notes. Since de Pas was short of money he published his etchings, badly annotated, on his own in 1623. When Menou de Charnizay found out what had happened, he went to the king and asked the permission to publish the book with a text he, Charnizay, would take care *of at the hand of the* notes. The result was two books, the first one published by de Pas with beautiful etchings under the name *Manége Royale*, and a second one published by Menou de Charnizay with the authentic text, but with bad illustrations, under the name *Instruction du Roy*. Because of the etchings of de Pas, later also used for the editions prepared by Charnizay, the book of Pluvinel received a great approval, more so than that of Salomon de la Broue, which was published in 1602. I think we can learn more from de la Broue, but his book did not have the beautiful pictures.

Rousselet, Jean (1783–1858)

After having taken part in most of the Napoleonic campaigns in Germany, Poland, Spain, Portugal and Russia, he received, in 1814, an appointment as instructor in Saumur. He had the reputation of being very kind with his horses; as one admirer said: "He spoke the language of the horses", and of being very patient with his pupils. He retired in 1849.

Seunig, Waldemar (1887–1976)

He was born in Laibach, Duchy of Krain, in the former Donau Monarchy. He was a descendant of traders and craftsmen who at the instigation of Maria-Theresia, Queen of Hungary, had emigrated to what is now Slowenia. The Seunigs developed into well-to-do landowning merchants in the town that is now called Llubljana.

After three years of Officers School in Wiener-Neustadt, Austria, he entered the cavalry in a Uhlan Regiment. First he was in Lemberg; then he went, after a few years to Olmütz, Moravia. In about 1911 he was sent to K. und K. Reitlehrer Institut, the imperial and royal School for future military riding instructors, in Vienna. There he became the pupil of Josipovich who would have a great influence on him. After four years of war on the Russian and Italian front, the government in Vienna told him to go to the country where he was born, Krain, and find something for himself. By that time, Krain had become part of Yugoslavia under the name of Slowenia. Since Seunig had made quite a name for himself as an outstanding rider and horseman, he was offered the job of Master of the Horse to the King of Yugoslavia. He accepted this offer under the condition that he first spend a year at the French military riding school in Saumur and after that half a year at the Royal Mews in London in order to learn the ceremonial and the protocol at the English Royal Court. After Seunig had organised the Royal Stables in Belgrade, he was granted a year to the Spanish Riding School in Vienna. At the end of the 1920s, the health of King Alexander deteriorated and he lost his interest in riding. The function of Master of the Horse diminished, and Seunig was offered the directorship of the newly founded military riding school. In 1933, when Seunig was up for promotion to become a general, he asked for his retirement. As a general, he would have been in command of a cavalry brigade; having no patriotic feelings for Yugoslavia, he did not think it appropriate to accept this command. After his retirement he kept riding, competing in several European countries, but he also started his literary career.

During the Second World War life for German-speaking people was very difficult in Slowenia, where he had settled in his ancestral mansion. The partisans burnt the house, so he fled to Germany . . . and entered the army. To those who criticise his second change of uniform, he had this to say: "The fact of my being German is not in the first place a mark of political conviction. It rather is a mark of human temperament and disposition; a special way to see things and to cope with them."

After the war Seunig travelled extensively, teaching and judging. In 1964 he came for the first time to the United States. In 1965 and in 1966 he was in Hawaii, California, the Midwest, British Columbia, Saskatchewan, Ontario and Vermont. A stroke in 1967 put an end to his travels.

His main work is *Von der Koppel bis zur Kapriole* (in English translation *Horsemanship*). A second book *Am Pulsschlag der Reitkunst* was published in English under the title *The Essence of Horsemanship* in 1983 (and reprinted in 1986).

Seunig had a style of writing seldom found in authors who write horse related books. He was poetic and picturesque, which often makes translation extremely difficult. Seunig's life was horses; his hobby was literature.

Simon of Athens

Born during the first quarter of the 5th century B C. Supposedly, he wrote the first book in the dialect of Attica. In this book he developed a system of equitation. The book is lost but for one chapter, dealing with the conformation of horses and the selection of them. We know about the contents of the whole book because Xenophon refers to it; so does Plinius the Elder, a Roman author. Savy de Lerville (*Von Olympia zum Olymp*) defends a thesis that Simon independently developed a system of horsemanship when he was assigned to resurrect a cavalry unit in Athens. For over a hundred years, there had been no cavalry in Athens; therefore, this unit had to be built up from scratch, and to do this in an organised way, Simon wrote what was to become the first cavalry manual, written around 450 B C. Since, according to the sources, Simon had a great reputation of being an excellent rider. Savy de Lerville points to the possibility that Simon's horses had been the models for the frieze of the

Parthenon. Against the theory that Xenophon had been involved with the sculptures, de Lerville stresses the fact that the frieze already existed when Xenophon was born.

Steinbrecht, Gustav (1808–85)

Son of a protestant minister, Steinbrecht was a veterinary student in Berlin when he started taking riding lessons from Louis Seeger, a pupil of the famous Oberbereiter in Vienna, Max von Weyrother. He married Seeger's niece and never left. He prepared horses for the circus, but contrary to Baucher, adhered strictly to classical principles. His posthumous book, *Das Gymnasium des Pferdes* goes directly back to la Guérinière and is still considered to be the fount of Germanic equitation.

Versailles, School of

In 1680, Louis XIV moved with his court to Versailles. The building of the palace, started during the reign of Louis XIII, had deen completed. Since the court moved constantly through the country, a lot of horses were needed to move not only the king with his family but also hundreds of courtiers with their dependents. The men generally rode, while the women were driven in carriages. In 1682, the horses were moved to their new stables in Versailles. There were two, La Grande Écurie and La Petite Écurie, the big and the small stables. The big stable was for riding horses and the small stable for the king's horses, the carriage horses, hunters and post-horses. At one time, there were 4,000 horses in the big stables and 800 people were employed there. For the small stables the figures were about 60 riding horses and 300 coach horses, with 300 employees. In charge of all this was the "Grand Écuyer", generally called Monsieur le Grand. Since the 11th century those in charge of stables had gradually improved their status in the court hierarchy. When they had reached the summit and had become "Grand Écuyer", they had nobody above them but the king. The charge of the "Grand Écuyer", encompassed not only the royal stables, but also the royal stud-farm. He licensed those who taught in the riding academies, and he also was responsible for all the buying of the horses for the government. Both the Grande and the Petite Écurie were run by an "Écuyer Commandant", both of them assisted by several "écuyers ordinaires" and "écuyers cavalcadours". The last category were in charge of schooling the horses of the king and the princes.

The "Grand Écurie"

The place where the School of Versailles was born. The kings of France were always above average riders; some of them were passionate followers of hounds. And all had a great interest in artistic equitation. This interest made them spend large amounts of money to encourage this equitation. As a result, the riders could concentrate without any material worries on the development of this artistic equitation, which, because of the dedicated concentration of the most talented riders, became classical equitation. The same happened in Austria, where the "Spanische Hofreitschule" until 1918 belonged to the imperial court.

Xenophon (c. 430–c. 355 BC)

He was involved in the Pelopponesian war; after that, he joined Cyrus in his ill-fated campaigning against Artaxerxes. After the debacle, he led his 10,000 men through Asia Minor to the Black Sea. After more fighting in Thrace and Phrygia, he settled in 387 with his wife, a Greek from Asia Minor and his two sons in Scillonte, in the neighbourhood of Olympia. There he did most of his extensive writing. In this context, only his book about equitation and about the Cavalry commander are of interest. These books both have come to us intact. Therefore, it was presumed for a long time that Xenophon was the inventor of everything he describes, although he very often refers to Simon of Athens. Savy de Lerville has made it clear that we have to see Xenophon as the pupil and developer of Simon's ideas.

Bibliography

Albrecht, Kurt, *Bogmen der Reitkunst*. Orac-Pietsch, Wien, 1981.

Albrecht, Kurt, *Meilensteine auf dem Weg zur Hohen Schule*, Olms Presse, Hildesheim, 1983.

Albrecht, Kurt, *Dressurrichter*. Orac-Pietsch, Wien, 1976.

Amman, Max, *Geschichte des Pferdesports*. Bucher, Luzern.

Anderson, J. K., *Ancient Greek Horsemanship*. University of California Press, Los Angeles, 1961.

d'Aure, Antoine Cartier, *Cours d'Équitation*. Émile Hazan, Paris, 1962.

Baucher, François, *Dictionnaire d'Équitation*. Émile Hazan, Paris, 1966.

Baucher, François, *Méthode d'Équitation*. Librairie de Mezière, Paris, 1976.

Baucher, François, *The Principles of Horsemanship*. Vinton & Co., London, 1919.

Beudant, Étienne, *Extérieure et Haute Ecole*. Charles Amat, Paris, 1923.

Blendinger, Wilhelm, *Menschen, Pferde und Kultur*. Paul Parey, Berlin, 1981.

Boisseau, Jeanne, *Notes sur l'enseignement de Nuno Oliveira*. Crépin-Leblon, Paris, 1979.

Boldt, Harry, *Das Dressur Pferd*. Edition Haberbeck, Lage-Lippe, Paris, 1970.

de Bragance, Diogo, *l'Équitation de la tradition française*. Odége, Paris, 1975.

Burkner, Felix, *Ein Reiterleben*. Kornett Verlag, Verden-Aller, 1957.

Decarpentry, Albert, *Baucher et son école*. Lamarre, Paris, 1948.

Decarpentry, Albert, *Piaffer et Passage*, Oberthur, Rennes-Paris, 1932.

Decarpentry, Albert, *Équitation Academique*. Henri Neveu, Paris, 1949.

Decarpentry, Albert, *Academic Equitation*. J. A. Allen, London, 1971.

Challan Belval et Xavier Lesage, *Trois grands Écuyers de Manège de Saumur*.

Challan Belval, *Dressage*, Émile Hazan, Paris, 1964.

Chenevix-Trench, Charles, *A History of Horsemanship*, Longman, London, 1970.

Demko-Belansky, Tibor von, *So reitest Du*. Orac-Pietsch, Wien, 1973.

Dent, Anthony, *The Horse Through Fifty Centuries of Civilization*, Phaidon, London, 1974.

Dent, Anthony and Machin-Goodall, Daphne, *The Foals of Epona*. Galley Press, London, 1962.

Bibliography

Eisenberg, Baron von, *Die wohl eingerichtete Reitschule*. Olms Verlag, Hildesheim, 1974.

d'Endrödy, Agaston, *Give Your Horse a Chance*. J. A. Allen, London, 1959.

Faverot, de Kerbrech, *Dressage Méthodique*. Emile Hazan, Paris, 1958.

Fillis, James, *Journal de Dressage*. Flammarion, Paris, 1903.

v. Flotow and Rolf Becher, *Reitergedanken*. Sankt Georg, Berlin, 1938.

Frank, Oscar, *Reiten*. Schweizer Kavallerist, Pfäffikon, Zürich, 1970.

Frank and others. *Theoretisch gewuszt*. Schweizer Kavallerist Pfäffikon, Zürich, 1964.

French-Blake, Neil, *The World of Dressage*. Doubleday, New York, 1969.

Froissard, Jean, *Equitation*. Wilshire Book, Hollywood, 1972.

Fuchs, Karl Otto von, *Umgang mit Reittpferden* BLV, München, 1968.

Benoist-Gironière, Yves, *la Conquète du Cheval*. Champs Élysées, Paris, 1947.

Glahn, Erich, *Die Reitkunst am Scheideweg*. Erich Hoffmann, Heidenheim, 1956.

Glahn, Erich, *Die Weltreiterei und wir*.

Gogue, René, *Problèmes équestres*. Maloine, Paris, 1978.

Gordon, W. J., *The Horse World of London*, (1893). J. A. Allen, London.

Gossin, Danièle, *Psychologie et Comportement du cheval*. Maloine S.A., Paris, 1982.

Grisone, Federigo, *Gli Ordini di cavalcare*. Olms Presse, Hildesheim, 1972.

Gudin de Vallerin, Maurice, *Obstacle conduie et style*. Henri Neveu, Paris, 1950.

la Guérinière, François Robichon de, *École de Cavalerie*. Huart et Moreau, 1751.

Hançar, Franz, *Das Pferd in praehistorischer Zeir*. Herold, Wien, 1956.

Handler, Hans, *Die Spanische Hofreitschule*. Molder, Wien, 1972.

Harris, Charles, *Riding and Dressage*. Harris, London, 1981.

Hazlinszky, Geza von, *Dressuurryden, Protocol en Kritiek*. De Hoefslag den Haag.

Henriquet, Michel, *À la Recherche de l'Équitation*. Crépin-Leblond, Paris, 1968.

Henriquet, Michel, *Les Maîtres de l'Équitation classique*. André Gérard, Paris, 1974.

Herbermann, Erik F., Dressage Formula. J. A. Allen, London, 1978.

Heydebreck, Hans von, *Reitlehrer und Reiter*. Mittler und Sohn, Berlin, 1928.

Heydebreck, Hans von, *Das Gebrauchspferd*. Mittler und Sohn, Berlin, 1935.

Heydebreck, Hans von, *Die Deutsche Dressurprüfung*. Rudolf Georgi, Aachen, 1972.

Heyer, H. J., *Reflections on the Art of Horsemanship*. J. A. Allen, London, 1968.

l'Hotte, Alexis, *Officier de Cavalerie*. Émile Hazan, Paris, 1958.

l'Hotte, Alexis, *Questions Equestres*. Émile Hazan, Paris, 1960.

Hünersdorf, Ludwig, *Anleitung*. Olms Presse, Hildesheim, 1973.

Jankovich, Miklos, *Pferde, Reiter, Volkerstürme*. BLV, München.

Jonquère d'Oriola, Pierre, *A cheval sur cinq jolympiades*. Raoul Solar, 1968.

Joussaume, André, *Dressage*. Édition du fer à cheval, Paris, 1951.

Joussaume, André, *Progressive Dressage*. J. A. Allen, London, 1978.

Klimke, Reiner, *Military*. Franckh, Stuttgart, 1967.

Klimke, Reiner. *Grundausbildung des jungen Reitpferdes*. Franckh, Stuttgart, 1980.

Koch, Ludwig, *Die Reitkunst in Bilde*, 1925.

Kretschmar, Marit, *Pferd und Reiter im Orient*. Olms Presse, Hildesheim, 1980.

Kulesza, S. R., *Modern Riding*. Arco, New York, 1966.

Licart, Jean, *Basic Equitation*. J. A. Allen, London, 1968.

Loon, Ernest van, *Ruiters en Rechters*. Zuidgroep, den Haag, 1978.

Machin-Goodall, Daphne, *Pferde der Welt*. Erich Hoffmann, Heidenheim, 1966.

Mairinger, Franz, *Horses are made to be Horses*, Rigby, Sydney, 1983.

Margot, *Comment juger*. Fédération française des sports équestres, Paris, 1967.

Markham, Gervase, *The Complete Horseman*. Houghton Mifflin, Boston, 1975.

Mennessier de la Lance, *Bibliographie Hippique*. Nieuwkoop de Graaf, 1971.

Monteilhet, André, *Les Maîtres de l'oeuvre équestre*. Odége, Paris, 1979.

Müseler, Wilhelm, *Reitlehre*. Paul Parey, Berlin.

Newcastle, William Cavendish, Duke of, *General System of Horsemanship*. de Hoefslag den Haag, 1973.

Newcastle, William Cavendish, Duke of, *Nouvelle Méthode* (de Solleysel). Olms Presse, Hildesheim, 1973.

Oeynhausen, Christian von, *Abrichtung*. Olms Presse, Hildesheim, 1977.

Oliveira, Nuno, *Haute École*. J. A. Allen, London, 1965.

Oliveira, Nuno, *Réflexions sur l'art équestre*. Crépin-Leblond, Paris, 1965.

Oliveira, Nuno, *Reflections on Equestrian Art*. J. A. Allen, London, 1976.

Oliveira, Nuno, *Classical Principles of the Art of Riding*. Howley & Russell.

Olstef, Sobène, *De l'équitation, la méthode et ses principes.* Crépin-Leblond, Paris, 1978.

d'Orgeix, Jean, *Équitation.* Robert Lafont, Paris, 1977.

Pluvinel, Antoine de, *le Manège royal.* J. A. Allen, London, 1970.

Pluvinel, Antoine de, *l'Instruction du Roy.* Griff, Paris, 1976.

Podhajsky, Alois, *Die Spanische Hofreitschule.* Hans Hammer, Wien, 1948.

Podhajsky, Alois, *Ein Leben fur die Lipizzaner.* Nymphenburger, München, 1960.

Podhajsky, Alois, *Die Klassische Reitkunst.* Nymphenburger, München, 1965.

Podhajsky, Alois, *Meine Lehrmeister die Pferde.* Nymphenburger, München, 1967.

Podhajsky, Alois, *Reiten und Richten.* Nymphenburger, München, 1973.

Rau, Gustav, *Die Reitkunst der Welt.* Sankt Georg, Düsseldorf, 1937.

Saint-Fort Paillard, Jean, *l'Équitation.* Chiron Sport, Paris, 1974.

Saint-Phalle, Jacques de, *Dressage et emiloi du chevel de selle.* Crépin-Leblond, Paris, 1969.

Salins, Jean de, *Épaule en dedans.* Émile Hazan, Paris, 1957.

Santini, Piero, *Riding Reflexions. Country Life, London,* 1933.

Santini, Piero, *Caprilli Papers.* J. A. Allen, London, 1967.

Savy de Lerville, *Von Olympia zum Olymp.* Bengt Birck, München, 1972.

Saurel, Étienne, *Pratique de l'Équitation d'apres les Maîtres français.* Flammarion, 1964.

Saurel, Étienne, *Histoire de l'Équitation.* Stock, Paris, 1971.

Schäfer, Michael, *Wie werde ich Pferdekenner.* Nymphenburger, München, 1971.

Schäfer, Michael, *Die Sprache des Pferdes.* Nymphenburger, München, 1976.

Schäfer, Michael, *Mit Pferden leben.* Nymphenburger, München, 1982.

Schusdziarra, H. & V., *Gymnasium des Reiters.* Paul Parey, Berlin, 1978.

Seeger, Louis, *System der Reitkunst.* Olms Presse, Hildesheim, 1974.

Seherr-Thoss, H. von, *Dressurprüfungen.* M. & H. Schaper, 1967.

Seunig, Waldemar, *Von der Koppel bis zur Capriole.* Fritz und Wasmuth, Zürich, 1949.

Seunig, Waldemar, *Im Sattel zählte ich keine Zeit.* Sankt Georg, Düsseldorf, 1958.

Seunig, Waldemar, *Meister der Reitkunst.* Erich Hoffmann, Heidenheim, 1960.

Seunig, Waldemar, *Am Pulsslag der Reitkunst.* Erich Hoffmann, Heidenheim, 1961.

Seunig, Waldemar, *Horsemanship.* Doubleday, New York, 1956.

Bibliography

Steinbrecht, Gustav, *Das Gymnasium des Pferdes*. Rudolf Georgi, Aachen, 1966.

Steinbrecht, Gustav, *Le Gymnase du Cheval*. Epiac, Paris, 1963.

Vigneron, Paul, *Le Cheval dans l'Antiquité*. Annales de l'Est, Nancs, 1968.

Waring, George H., *Horse Behavior*. Noyes Publications, 1983.

Wätjen, Richard, L. *Das Dressurreiten*. Paul Parey, Berlin, 1975.

Weyrother, Max Ritter von, *Hinterlassene Schriften*. Olms Presse, Hildesheim, 1977.

Wiesener (and others), *Die Kulturen der eurasischen Volker*. Athenaion, Frankfurt am Main, 1968.

Wiesener, Joseph, *Fahren und Reiten in Alteuropa und im alten Orient*. Olms Presse, Hildesheim, 1971.

Wynmalen, Henry, *Equitation*. Country Life, London, 1938.

Wynmalen, Henry, *Dressage*. Wilshire, Hollywood, 1972.

Xenophon, *Scripta Minora*. Harvard, Cambridge, 1968.

Zeuner, Frederick F. *Geschichte der Haustiere*. BLV, München, 1967.